Seventy Thirty Exclusive Matchmaking

Expert opinion, tips, dating secrets and insights into the world of relationships by the leaders in exclusive matchmaking and psychology

Susie Ambrose

www.seventy-thirty.com

This book is dedicated with love to my amazing daughter Natalija, and to my wonderful brother Aleksandar, both of whom continue to inspire me.

'Love is composed of a single soul inhabiting two bodies.'

Aristotle

Contents

Testimonials

Acknowledgements

I would like to thank all the wonderful psychologists relationship experts who have helped with the work of Seventy Thirty over the past ten years, and who have greatly contributed to this book.

In particular, I would like to acknowledge Trudy Hill MSc, Lemarc Thomas BSc, Dr Rina Bajaj, Dr Briony Hudson, Dr Zilijeta Krivokapic, Melissa Agius MSc, Susan Eades MSc, Francesca Moresi MSc, Chelsea Thomas MSc and Zoya Siddiqui MA.

Thanks also go to Michael Andreas and Jonathan Harrison for supporting my vision for Seventy Thirty.

Finally, I acknowledge and thank some of my incredible clients, who wished to share their coaching experience and relationship questions in this book. All names have been changed in the interests of confidentiality.

PREFACE

THE BIRTH OF SEVENTY THIRTY

I grew up in rural Yugoslavia, under Communist rule. Guided by my parents, a professional couple who encouraged independence and creativity, I quickly developed a strong entrepreneurial drive. As the threat of war loomed, I decided to move to London to begin a new life. I arrived with about £30 in my pocket, not knowing anyone here and speaking hardly any English. However, being assertive and hard-working, I found the challenge exciting. I appreciated England and the opportunities it offered to me and so, after training as a psychoanalyst and working within the NHS, I opened my own psychotherapy clinic.

While running my psychotherapy practice, I noticed that many of my clients were wealthy and attractive, yet, because of their busy lifestyles they had difficulty in meeting a compatible partner. At this time, an aristocratic gentleman came to me looking for help to find love. I decided to help him. Successfully matching him with a woman he loved and respected was the catalyst that drove me to build Seventy Thirty. It is now a globally recognised, elite matchmaking agency staffed by a team of psychologists and relationship experts and with a membership of remarkable single people.

My focus has always been on building a matchmaking agency that delivers what it promises: a brand built through positive word-of-mouth reviews. I had enough contacts within my network to launch the service, and I started by making select introductions myself. Seventy Thirty's young, dynamic psychologists have a genuine passion for helping our members find meaningful connections and long-lasting love.

The name 'Seventy Thirty' came about after I read a study which found that successful people spend around 70% of their time working and 30% socialising. A decade later, Seventy Thirty is the epitome of luxury and power, the leading exclusive matchmaking company providing world-class services around the globe.

The second ingredient differentiating Seventy Thirty from other agencies and drawing clients from all over the world (many of whom charter a flight to London just to meet us) is our focus on finding exceptional partners for our exceptional members; someone with whom they will find lasting love.

Susie Ambrose, August 2014

FOREWORD

This book explains how to find and maintain a loving relationship built on honesty, trust and respect. In the course of the work and research undertaken by Seventy Thirty, my team of psychologists and I have met thousands of amazing people, who have given us a solid and thorough understanding of human relationships.

In this book we reveal some of our best-kept secrets about how to be your own matchmaker. We have spent ten intensive years matchmaking for men and women. People often ask us, 'How do you matchmake so well?' and 'How do you actually go about matchmaking?' This book will answer these questions and many more.

In this book, we give examples of questions to ask potential dates; offer advice on when certain questions should be asked; and tell you why it's important to be open to all types of people, not just your 'ideal' or normal type.

The most important point is that you need to make sure your partner is compatible with you, using the four main parameters we use when we matchmake: background, lifestyle, sexual attraction and relationship goals. Of course, there are also other factors to consider, such as socio-economic status, family, and political and religious values.

From antiquity to the modern day, dating has established itself as a ritual, which we have long considered as the precursor to assessing the suitability of a potential life partner. From an evolutionary perspective, the notion of 'dating' – that is, courtship or wooing – is actually a relatively recent phenomenon. In the past, the focus was on sexual reproduction to produce genetically viable offspring, therefore strengthening the family lineage. From a historical standpoint, dating existed only to the extent to which a couple-to-be was first introduced before, or at, their wedding ceremony. Indeed, many cultures still don't condone dating, choosing instead to have a system of arranged marriages, whereby relationships are based on factors such as family, status and lineage.

The first decade of the 20th century in western culture saw the beginning of our modern interpretation of 'dating'. During this time, it was usual for parents to use their social networks or involve matchmakers to find potential suitors for their sons and daughters. Dates were then arranged, with the parents' permission and in the presence of an all-divulging chaperone. The couple was seldom left unaccompanied, so they had very little opportunity for intimacy or carnal exchange. However, many people were unable to dedicate their resources to finding partners in this way, and over time people's – and society's – attitude changed towards male–female relationships, so dating became more of an individual choice.

The past century also saw a number of social changes, such as the introduction of birth control (oral contraceptive pills), active women's rights movements, and the legalisation of abortion, which together have fundamentally changed the dating landscape. Today, while the number-one priority for most people is a long-term commitment, such as marriage, both men and women also value their independence, have their own goals and ambitions, and are more willing to remain single until they find the right person for them.

Changes in society have led to more modern ways of meeting potential partners, such as introduction and dating agencies. Today's single people have many options to find the right person, and by being proactive they are very likely to meet someone special.

PART ONE: Understanding human relationships

1. Can having a positive attitude directly impact the success of your relationships?

In addition to the potential health benefits of positive thinking, this approach to life can also help to improve your relationships with others. People like to be around people who are positive. A shared sense of humour has been shown to improve resilience in relationships, as well as communication; people are more relaxed when they laugh and are able to express their true feelings and release any pent-up emotions (such as anger) in a more positive way, which is more likely to lead to greater levels of trust and intimacy within your relationship.

By having a positive attitude to a relationship and being relaxed, you are more likely to make your partner feel happy and loved, as positivity is contagious! Being positive will also help you to cope more easily with any stressors in a relationship.

2. The importance of kindness in relationships

The golden rule of treating others as you would like to be treated by them is a concept that, when practised, allows us to reap rewards in our relationships. Further, by being kind to others we are inadvertently also helping ourselves; improving our mood, strengthening our self-respect and confidence and making ourselves more attractive to others.

From an evolutionary perspective, the development and adoption of this rule make sense. We are social animals, we live in groups, so reciprocity in caring behaviours, involving emotions such as empathy and compassion, to other members of our group is something that can only help our species to survive. Of course, to be motivated to effectively practise this behaviour requires us to have a healthy view of ourselves as equally deserving of receiving kindness from others.

Supporting this theoretical perspective is neuroscientific research that suggests our ability to treat others with kindness is actually hardwired into our brains. Research by Dr Marco Iacobini[1] found that our brains contain 'mirror neurons' that automatically fire when we observe actions of others, prompting us to naturally empathise with them; in other words, to feel what they are feeling. Firing of these neurons only ceases when we attribute a negative

---

[1] Iacobini, M. (2009) Imitation, empathy and mirror neurons. *Annual Reviews in Psychology, 60,* 653–70.

label to the other person that dampens our empathic response.

Further, kindness can also be learned through a process of conditioning. When we are kind to others we are rewarded by the release of a cocktail of neurochemicals, such as oxytocin, serotonin and dopamine. These are known to improve our mental and physical wellbeing. This improvement in our mood then reinforces the likelihood that we will repeat that behaviour.

So, why do I say that kindness can improve our attractiveness to others? Research has found that kindness and warmth are the most desirable traits in any type of relationship, and are considered even more important than physical attractiveness when selecting a romantic partner.

Professor Arthur Aron,[2] whose research interests including discovering determinants of successful long-term romantic relationships, states that being attractive 'doesn't help that much', suggesting that people tend to fall in love more readily with kind people. Further, he argues that kindness is the strongest indicator for a successful long-term relationship.

Decades of research by the Gottman Institute, an organisation that helps couples to build and maintain healthy relationships, goes some way to explaining why

---

[2] Aron, A. (2005) Why do we fall in love? (10 May). At: http://health.howstuffworks.com/relationships/love/why-do-we-fall-in-love.htm.

these traits are important. This may appear obvious, but they found that, in order for relationships to flourish, both parties' emotional needs have to be met, and that 'interaction styles' involving kindness and generosity rather than contempt and disinterest are preferred. Observing the interaction styles of couples has enabled psychologists at the Institute to predict, with a 94% rate of accuracy, whether couples will remain together or not.

There are a number of ways that we can become kinder:

• To ensure that our future is not unduly influenced by past negative experiences, we can practise forgiveness and tolerance towards others – as well as to ourselves – for things that have happened to us.

• We can give our time to others less fortunate than ourselves, perhaps through volunteering.

• We can demonstrate random acts of kindness to those whom we are either connected or unconnected to.

• We can express gratitude to those who have shown us kindness.

Being kind to others does not mean that you should be taken for granted, and it is important to recognise that there are some individuals for whom no amount of kindness will prompt them to similarly respond to you, respect you or even like you. Being kind doesn't mean that you sacrifice your needs for the needs of others. You can be kind *and* assertive; they are not mutually exclusive traits.

The important point to remember is that, by being kind, you are respecting yourself and can be proud of your behaviour. Also, you are increasing your own attractiveness by being both kind and positive.

3. What makes a modern relationship work?

At Seventy Thirty, we are in the fortunate position of having the opportunity to speak to thousands of men and women about what *they* think makes a relationship work. Here are some of the main themes that are most commonly cited as important to ensure a successful relationship.

Each partner in the relationship should have an equal contributing role. There should be a balance in what two parties contribute to the relationship in order to create a workable status quo. You do not have to contribute the *same* things; the key is to show that you are putting in as much as you want to receive in terms of love, support and communication. Problems can arise in a relationship when one person perceives that they are giving more than they are receiving.

Have clear and honest relationship goals. By establishing goals such as, 'I want to find a long-term, committed relationship', 'I want to get married and start a family', or 'I want to enjoy myself and not get tied down just yet', a person will know what they are looking for in a partner and can focus their attention and effort on finding the right person. By being honest with yourself and potential partners (and getting the same in return), you will not waste time in unfulfilling relationships.

Both partners should feel some level of control. Clearly defining shared goals as a couple and working out the necessary steps towards achieving these will influence the direction you are heading in. There is also some psychology behind this. Creating joint goals allows us to feel a greater sense of control, so that we feel more secure in our relationship.

What makes us want to stay with someone for the long term can be very different to what makes us start a relationship. Real love is based on friendship combined with attraction – shared backgrounds, shared value systems and similar moral codes, mutual understanding and shared relationship goals. People are extremely social creatures and we want someone who we can communicate with, someone who will support us, who we can laugh with and share our lives with.

4. How do you become attractive to the opposite sex?

We know that attraction is an important element of a relationship, but men and women find different things attractive. Here are some tips for creating that spark.

What men want:

- Positivity – men prefer someone who has a positive outlook on life and sees the glass as half-full rather than half-empty.
- Drive and ambition; a 'go-getter' attitude – even if you aren't where you want to be yet, men tend to appreciate focus and determination.
- Independence – men are often attracted to women who are independent and have their own interests, as this helps to maintain a balance in a relationship.
- Intelligence – men tend to look for someone who is their equal, both mentally and emotionally. Men like to be able to hold an intelligent conversation with their partner. Emotional stability is key; you need to be emotionally whole going into a relationship to ensure that you are in the relationship because you *want* to be, rather than because you *need* to be. There should be a good degree of emotional compatibility.
- Confidence and self-esteem – most men find confidence and self-esteem highly attractive traits.

What women want:

- Leadership – many women prefer men who are charismatic; someone who is a leader and not afraid to express himself.
- Confidence – most women find confidence extremely sexy. This is not to be confused with arrogance or dominance! It is more to do with having a 'can do'

attitude and a willingness to keep trying when the going gets tough.

- Old-fashioned values – many women value old-fashioned values such as helpfulness and politeness.
- Passion to succeed – women often look for a man who is successful in his own right. This may mean that he is following his passion in life. From the perspective of evolutionary psychology, successful men (or men who have the potential to become successful, through their ambition and drive) are preferred as mates and long-term partners.
- Equality – women want a balanced relationship, in which they feel appreciated and valued. For most women, an equal balance of power within a relationship is the key to its success.
- Ability to express emotions – women value emotional expression, as it is a crucial step towards developing intimacy within a relationship.
- Similarity – women tend to be more attracted to people who are similar to them; this can be in terms of occupation, values and lifestyle.
- A sense of fun – women tend to value partners who are fun and adventurous.

When looking for a long-term partner, both men and women look for people with a sense of humour, and who are friendly and communicative, as these traits all help to form compatible and cooperative relationships.

5. Attachment and separation issues – the human dilemma

Psychologist John Bowlby's attachment theory states that an infant needs to develop a relationship with at least one primary caregiver for the child's successful social and emotional development, and in particular for learning how to effectively regulate their feelings. According to this theory, then, the relationship we have, as infants, have with our caregivers has a big impact on the choices we make in relationships as adults. In other words, it can drive our adult relationship choices on an unconscious level.

One recognised attachment style is 'disorganised attachment', which generally occurs in infants who have a difficult relationship with their parents; one example is parents who have abusive or inconsistent parenting styles, so that the child does not know what to expect. If this is not addressed, the result in adulthood is an individual who both craves and is mistrustful of close bonds with others; adults with disorganised attachment may want to achieve real emotional closeness with a partner, but fear that opening up and getting too close to someone will then give a partner the power to reject them and hurt them. Disorganised attachment can be very confusing for both the person and also their partner.

Practical help – how to heal from disorganised attachment

If you know that you want to meet someone but you are afraid to open up, try to recognise that you stand a much greater chance of creating and maintaining a successful relationship if you develop healthy boundaries from the outset. If you are in a new relationship, learn to be emotionally available so that you are able to give and receive love, but at the same time ensure you don't develop a co-dependent relationship, where you don't feel capable and competent as a person in your own right.

It's important to understand that negative thought patterns and behaviour can be hard to unlearn. However, remember that no one is perfect! We all have parts of ourselves that we are dislike or we would like to improve. Think positively, and treat others with the same respect that you would want to receive. Counselling from a therapist experienced in attachment issues is often hugely beneficial in these situations.

6. The language of love: enhancing emotional communication in romantic relationships

The language of love: do you speak it? We all know that communication, both verbal and non-verbal, is crucial in our relationships. It is essential that both partners in a romantic relationship have a shared understanding of the meanings inherent in the messages and behaviours expressed by the other. In short, they must be speaking the same language.

But when it sometimes seems as if you and your partner are from different planets, how can you achieve this? The answer may lie in Dr Gary Chapman's acclaimed book, *The Five Love Languages: How to Express Heartfelt Commitment to Your Mate*. Chapman suggests that every individual has a 'primary love language' and, in order to feel truly loved and valued in a relationship, this love must be expressed to the individual directly in line with their categorised love language. Verbal or non-verbal, the key to success in all interpersonal relationships is the *expression* and *receipt* of love. To feel cherished by our partner, it is important that love is communicated to them in ways that they understand.

Chapman distinguishes between five love languages, noting that each language entails a certain way of expressing and receiving love, which should be tailored specifically to the needs and desires of the individual. Based on mutual reciprocity, the critical point is to ensure long-lasting love; not only should you learn to speak your partner's love language, but you must be fully fluent.

The five love languages are:

Words of affirmation: Individuals for whom this is their primary love language experience love through the receipt of verbal forms of emotional support, praise or encouragement. Being told 'I love you', hearing the reasons why they are loved and receiving unsolicited compliments are prized above all non-verbal gestures of love. It is noteworthy that, for these people, verbal insults and hurtful remarks can be devastating and are not easily forgotten.

Acts of service: These individuals feel loved when their partner does practical things that help them. In other words, actions speak louder than words for these individuals and they appreciate demonstrations of practical help and support.

Receiving gifts: The effort and sentiment behind a carefully selected gift or everyday gesture make these individuals feel cherished. Gifts are thus interpreted as showing that their partner is thinking of them, cares for them and understands their likes and needs. Consequently, a missed birthday present or inappropriate card would be an issue for these people.

Quality time: Individuals whose primary language is quality time experience love through the receipt of someone's time and undivided attention. They feel loved when they have a sense of togetherness with their partner, irrespective of the activity, as long as they are focused on one another.

Physical touch: This is the language of individuals who experience love through their partner's physical presence and contact. These individuals interpret appropriate physical touch and proximity to their partner as signs of care, support and affection. Neglect or physical abuse is therefore highly destructive to people for whom this is their love language.

According to the love languages model, different people 'speak' different love languages and, as is the case with the spoken word, it is easier to communicate in one's own native language. You can adapt your natural tendencies to ensure you express love in ways your partner understands and prefers, and this may ultimately be seen as greater expressions of love, thanks to your effort. Your partner should also try to communicate with you in *your* love language – the best relationships are based on communication and equal respect.

It is important to note that within the five distinct love languages there are innumerable ways of expressing love, so you can be as creative as you like and are limited only by your imagination! Furthermore, as with all forms of language acquisition, the more you use your partner's love language the more comfortable and proficient you will become in this secondary language.

For example, if your partner's love language is quality time, you simply need to make a conscious effort to give this to them, and they need to apply the same understanding and effort to express love in your language. When both partners alter their behaviour to fall in line with the other's, both partners will feel more loved, happy and secure. The simplicity of this reasoning does not undermine its potential power. As stated above, when in a loving relationship, it is important that both partners show and are shown this love. Therefore, when the main difficulty in a relationship is the surface-level communication of love, these simple behavioural changes could lead to massive improvements in the relationship.

This novel conceptualisation of emotional communication within relationships therefore has significant implications for those who wish to make their relationships more mutually fulfilling and rewarding. The book may also be helpful for people going through difficult periods in their relationships, and also provides valuable insights for people who are single and want to develop more meaningful relationships with future partners.

The concept does not focus on understanding and exploring the emotions that underlie people's need for love to be expressed in particular ways; it does not address deeper emotional problems within a relationship. Consequently, it does not teach people how to love and connect with their partner on a more fundamental level. The ideas in the book are not a 'fix all' remedy for all relationship problems, but rather a positive and practical way of enhancing an already-loving relationship.

Using and applying love languages can greatly enhance even the best relationships by ensuring that both partners know that they are loved, so reading this book may help you to improve your relationships.

7. Social politics, wealth and relationships

Why, when a wealthy woman dates a much younger attractive man, is she judged so much more than when a man does the same thing?

Today we are constantly bombarded by information. Social psychologists hypothesise that, in order to deal with this flow of information efficiently, we use subconscious templates to help us make judgements about the people and things we encounter. These templates, known as *schemata*, help us to slot people and things quickly into nice, neat categories so that we know how to respond to them.

This is generally helpful for things that we are familiar with, but when we come across unfamiliar people or situations, these schemata can cause us trouble. We are forced to make new schemata to accommodate this new information – and the new schemata may not always be positive or even correct. Our schemata define what we consider to be normal, in terms of people, behaviours and even relationships, allowing us to feel that we understand them and the world in which we live. For example, in our society, we have schemata for what we consider 'normal' in sexual relationships between couples, which is generally defined as being between people of similar ages. Additionally, our society generally shares schemata for relationships between older, wealthy men and younger, beautiful women. Because we have schemata for these relationships, we accept them as normal and do not pay them too much attention.

According to social psychology, things that seem unfamiliar are likely to be regarded with suspicion, and often fear. These feelings stem from the potential that 'unusual' information has to make us question our understanding of the world, and our place within it. Humans tend to crave understanding, and the sense of control that comes with it. Indeed, the less we understand something, the more we fear it.

Perhaps this is the reason why relationships between older women and younger men tend to be judged more negatively than their reverse. Our collective lack of schemata for this relationship dynamic means that this type of relationship is considered 'abnormal' and therefore frightening.

As schemata are driven by culture and society, they differ across the world. For example, in many well-known tourist spots there tend to be more older women seeking the company of younger men. Indeed, some western women travel to these locations specifically for this purpose. As such, this relationship dynamic is absorbed into the norms and schemata of this culture. It is considered normal and raises no eyebrows. Often the most upwardly mobile eyebrows belong to those who do not share the schemata of the local residents.

If we think about the question from an evolutionary perspective, and understand that, as well as being rooted in social norms, our behaviour is also driven by the innate knowledge we have gathered over millennia of evolution, we get another take on it. A relationship between an older man and a younger woman makes sense from an evolutionary viewpoint. This relationship would achieve the goals of both parties: she would provide him with children and he would in turn deliver the resources and protection she requires.

From this perspective we can understand why women have a tendency to be attracted to power. Increased power means increased access to resources. Power enables the male to provide for potential offspring and means that he will be able to select a healthy mother for his children, so they will benefit from a strong and healthy gene pool. Viewed through this lens, it is not surprising that – even today – men can offset their power against other elements of attraction (in which they may be lacking, such as appearance and age) to attract a young and healthy woman.

Inversely, historically, men are not as sexually attracted to power, and tend to prefer to obtain power through competition with other males, rather than their selection of a mate. Unfortunately, from a female perspective, this means that a powerful woman does not enjoy the same benefits from power as males in terms of increasing their attractiveness and compensating for other areas of attraction in which they may be lacking. This is likely to be another reason why the dynamic of older, powerful females and younger males may be harder to understand than its reverse. However, the world is evolving quickly. The rise in equality between men and women in terms of wealth and power and the subsequent increase in independent, successful women is changing the way society views traditional female norms. Over time, as this relationship type becomes assimilated into our culture and lives, schemata will develop and this relationship type will seem less unusual.

8. The science of love

Even when a relationship doesn't work out, they say, it is better to have loved and lost than never to have loved at all. Love, after all, is a powerful force. When people fall in love they may experience physical symptoms, such as feeling like doing something impulsive, finding it hard to concentrate, losing their appetite or their focus at work, or finding their priorities have changed. They may have less interest in friends and family, or spend time daydreaming, desperately waiting for their phone to ring. When we fall in love, our brains react to a number of different chemical changes. Brain imaging has also shown that when we fall in love our frontal cortex tends to shut down. This is the part of the brain that is vital to judgement, which is why we might act a little out of character. To add to this state, the anterior cingulated cortex is activated, which is associated with feelings of euphoria. Yes, this cocktail of chemicals is the natural high that we are all seeking.

However, this state does not last for ever. We know that passionate love tends to fade over time. Couples often worry that they don't feel the same as they did when they first met, and that something might have changed. This is not bad news; *au contraire*! After the honeymoon phase of a relationship, which usually lasts six months to a year, our brain's reaction to the chemicals mentioned above decreases, allowing us to enter a calmer, longer-lasting phase of our relationship.

PART TWO: Finding the right one

9. Are you ready for dating?

Although the differences between work and relationships are very apparent, those of us new or returning to the world of dating, via introduction agencies or matchmaking agencies, can still learn a lot from some of the similarities. People who have enjoyed successful careers are already equipped with many of the tools they need to thrive in the dating world. How so? Well, when you think about your career you will realise that, at some point, you took a good look at your own skills and motivations so that you were able to identify opportunities as they arose. You made an effort to dress appropriately for a role, promotion or interview. You took advice on interview techniques. You asked for feedback about yourself from previous employers or after an interview. Although you most certainly don't want to treat love as if it were a business, you probably have more skills than you realise that you can use to your advantage, and this will increase your success in dating. Later in this book, you will hear more from the experts at Seventy Thirty about finding love and making it work.

Dating takes time and energy, so it's important to know what you are looking for in a person. In the same way that you choose a job based what you would like to do, you need to take some time to think about the kind of person you would prefer to date; what you want out of a relationship and what you hope your partner will bring to a relationship.

First impressions count! Only 3% of communication is based on language; the other 97% is based on appearance, body language, tone of voice and rapport. If you are not confident about your appearance, manner and dating etiquette, ask an expert, previous men or woman you have dated, or a good friend for feedback on your dress, appearance and approach. Once you know where your weaknesses are, you will be able to strengthen them. Most people have asked for interview feedback in the world of work and learned from it, so applying the same approach to dating makes sense.

Confidence is extremely attractive to both men and women. It's vital to approach dating from a place of confidence and security if you want to enhance and showcase your attractiveness. Many people know what their strengths are in an office environment but are completely unaware of how important this same knowledge is for successful dating. So ask friends, family and, most importantly, yourself what it is that makes you special, and be sure to take the positive feedback on board.

We find ourselves most attracted to people who lead well-rounded and fulfilling lives rather than people who have put life 'on hold' until they find a partner. Perhaps it's time to start doing some of the things you have been putting off for later, such as travelling, learning new skills and socialising.

Do not shy away from taking the initiative to ensure you are in a position to meet the right calibre of single person. Put yourself out there and find ways to increase your opportunities to meet the type of people you want to meet. Be proactive. After all, you don't land your dream job without doing something to find it.

10. What is attraction?

Attraction is an important part of a relationship, but what defines attraction is more than simply physical appearance. Factors such as proximity, similarity and familiarity can also play an important part in making someone attractive. In terms of proximity, we tend to like people who we see every day, so you may start to notice someone who works in your building or sits in the same carriage on the Tube each morning. Another important element is similarity. We tend to be more attracted to people who are similar to us; this may be in terms of occupation, personality, background, intelligence, values and lifestyle. For a relationship to last, a couple needs to have a similar outlook on life, and both may need to make compromises by adjusting their life goals. Need to give an example of what you mean here? Life goals include things like having/not having children, working full time/not working, saving/not saving, and so on.

This can explain why shared values are so important in helping to keep the attraction alive in a long-term relationship.

11. Why is self-confidence attractive?

Attractiveness is down to more than just a pretty face. However, we usually consider our physical appearance first when deciding whether or not we are attractive.

Women tend to keep a close eye on their weight; on average, they spend £36,000 on hair care over their lifetime. Men tend to think about their stature, physique and hairline. We all have a tendency to focus on our appearance without realising that the pivotal factor in attractiveness is something entirely different: self-confidence.

When someone is confident, they transform the energy in a room. People are drawn to them; we want to be their friend, to talk to them – and to date them. In the world of dating, confidence is essential. Someone who doubts their own appearance and ability sends signals of insecurity that warn potential partners away. Self-assured individuals are looking for people who are as happy and healthy as they are. Confidence lures people in and reflects one's essence. If you are dreary and dull, people will want to avoid you. If you are bright and vibrant, people will want to be around you.

Academics confirm that a self-confident person has a real sense of who they are. They will come into a relationship 'whole', not in need of constant affirmations. Those who lack confidence depend on others' approval to feel good about themselves; this can be draining and unappealing.

Being confident puts you in a better position to manage the challenges and negotiations that a relationship brings. A self-confident person is aware of their imperfections, is comfortable with them and does not let them get in their way. Even the most confident people have bad days, but a positive attitude helps to give off an air of assurance that most people find attractive.

There is, however, a thin line between confidence and arrogance. Overconfidence is a definite turn-off. The quietly confident, self-assured person who is not afraid to show their vulnerability usually wins over the brash self-assurance of the overconfident.

Whether you are looking for that perfect partner or are already in a loving relationship, one must not underestimate the role of self-confidence. Finding or maintaining love always begins with the belief that you are worthy of love. Indeed, there is much truth to the cliché, 'before someone can love you, you have to love yourself!'

12. Mindfulness and relationship success

Imagine this.

You are dancing, feeling self-conscious, aware of your body and of other people watching. You feel stiff and fidgety and you can't enjoy yourself but you have to carry on because you have started.

Now imagine a second scenario.

You are dancing: you feel as free as a bird, there is a huge smile on your face, you feel the music and you move without thinking. You are not consciously aware of your body or other people watching; you are just having a good time.

In the first scenario, you are not being mindful. In the second one, you are.

Buddhist monks began to practise mindfulness more than 2,500 years ago. Mindfulness is essentially a state of heightened awareness of and attention to the present moment, while taking a non-judgemental and non-evaluative approach to one's experience. This is also important for successful dating. Living 'in the moment', which defines mindfulness, can be useful for promoting success and enhancing higher-quality romantic relationships. Mindfulness has been positively correlated with higher marital satisfaction, empathic concern, effective communication and adaptive response skills when faced with relationship stress.

As well as relationship satisfaction, mindfulness approaches have also been associated with increased sexual satisfaction. Women who practise mindfulness often say it allows them to be more aware and present during sex.

So often, we have so much on our mind that we forget to be mindful and live in the present; we allow time to rush past, unobserved and unseized. We squander the precious seconds of our lives as we worry about the future and dwell on the past. When we are not in a relationship, we fantasise about meeting that perfect partner; when we meet someone, we fear that we are missing out. We give in to intrusive memories of the past, or fret about what may or may not happen in the future.

In comparison, mindful people focus on making the present work. They tend to have higher self-esteem, are more accepting of their own weaknesses, fight less with their romantic partners, are more accommodating and less defensive. As a result, mindful couples have more satisfying relationships. People who are mindful focus on enjoying the moment they are in and making that be the best it can be.

13. Chemistry, psychology and immediate attraction

Why do we find ourselves immediately attracted to some people, but not others? What is this chemistry that people talk about as being an essential part of the development of any romantic relationship, and is chemistry the whole picture?

To begin to explore the first question, one needs to take a quick dip into the complicated world of neuroscience. Neuroscientific research uses brain-imaging techniques to identify the complex system of chemical messengers, neurotransmitters and hormones that are activated in certain parts of the brain when we see an object that we desire.

When we are attracted to someone, hormones are activated in our brain, which have an influence over the more rational, decision-making parts of our brain, which helps explain why it is sometimes difficult to think clearly when we are very attracted to someone. There is indeed *real* chemistry involved in attraction.

14. Relationship expectations

Everybody has ideas or expectations about their 'ideal' or 'perfect' partner and how they envisage their perfect relationship, and this is entirely natural. Our relationships form such a large part of our lives that we are bound to dream about what they should be like. However, when these ideas or rules become fixed or are unrealistic, we are automatically slamming the door in the face of many wonderful people and experiences. And when our rules or expectations are grounded in fantasy, rather than reality, they can be extremely damaging.

For example, we all want to desire – and be desired by – our partner. However, attraction is not based on physical appearance alone. A huge number of factors play a part in how attractive someone is, such as their confidence, intelligence, the way they hold themselves, the way they move, speak, or even smell. You cannot predict who you will have chemistry with, and you may end up feel that spark with someone who isn't your 'ideal', or even close to it. Having a specific physical formula for a partner rarely works, and having tunnel vision means potentially missing someone who is exciting in a way you may not expect.

It's not only expectations about a partner's physical appearance that can damage your chances of finding a soul mate. Many people develop a multitude of expectations that culminate in a lengthy checklist of 'essentials' that the perfect partner must have. However, it's important to realise which must-haves (such as respect and trust) are essential for a long-term relationship and which may need to be flexible (such as being funny or dressing in a certain way).

Expecting your partner to be perfect all the time is a recipe for disaster. Envision your 'perfect partner' as someone who is truly compatible with you, not someone who is perfect within themselves or in terms of your expectations. Remember, your partner is human too; they can't be there for you all the time, they will make mistakes, sometimes they will want to spend time with their friends rather than you, sometimes you will argue. Having some conflict is normal; it's how we resolve difficulties that is important. Expecting perfection all the time will doom the relationship to failure before it has even begun.

Don't expect the honeymoon period to last forever. Chemistry does fade; scientists have even managed to track this. They believe it to be a hardwired 'love' response that evolved because it kept two people together long enough for their offspring to survive. If you want a fulfilling, long-term relationship you should try to separate chemistry from compatibility and ensure that you have enough of both.

Finding the 'right' man or woman will not fix your life or complete you, despite what we see in the movies. However, the right partner will be able to provide you with the love and support you need for a healthy and happy life together. To achieve this, however, you need to accept that no couple is happy 100% of the time. Being content in yourself is the key to having realistic expectations of your partner. When you are happy in yourself, you are in a better position to think about what your partner can expect from you.

15. Finding true riches

What does being rich mean to you? Having £1 million, £1 billion, or more in your bank account? Having the freedom and flexibility to never have to take orders from someone else? Having more time to spend with your family? Travelling the world in style? Giving back to society in some way?

Take a moment to think about what being rich means to you. How would your life actually change and, more importantly, what would you want *not* to change?

We are all already rich in our own ways. We tend to have the things in our life that we value the most. Leading a rich life means recognising this and acknowledging the control we have. Through self-awareness, we can nurture a positive attitude towards the life that we have created. It is only when we realise that we have the things that are most important to us that we are able to see how fortunate we truly are.

16. Are you happy being single?

According to evolutionary theory, the fundamental purpose of life is reproduction. We are therefore 'pre-programmed' to find a compatible partner, reproduce and raise our children.

This is, of course, greatly oversimplified and in the modern world, where many other factors come into play (such as career, travel, money, health issues, personal choice etc.), it is not now the case that all we must do, or desire to do, in life is find a partner and raise a family.

Human beings are naturally social and companionable, and enjoy being in relationships. However, not being in a romantic relationship is not the end of the world! Being single is not a terminal illness – yet many people view it this way.

Why single people may feel unfulfilled or unhappy:

- *Social stigma* – they feel that society is more geared towards couples, and they feel ostracised as a single person.
- *Media pressure* – images of 'perfect' couples, happy marriages, etc. are represented as the norm and people therefore feel that, if they are single, they are somehow abnormal.
- *Concerns for their future* – inevitably, if they want to start a family and don't have a partner with whom to do so, they may feel under time pressure (this is particularly true for women who, unfortunately, have biological limits to their fertility).
- *Reduced social activity* – many single people dislike or feel unable to enter certain social environments or pursue certain social activities alone (e.g. 'I can't go on my own to the cinema/restaurant/concert').

Why single people should instead feel positive and hopeful:

- There is nothing wrong with being single, and just because you don't have a partner it does not mean you are not normal. Being single does not say anything negative about you personally, but merely reflects your present circumstances, which could change at any time.
- The media gives false impressions of *many* aspects of life (not just relationships); for instance, we are surrounded by images of people with 'dream' jobs, 'ideal' bodies, 'flawless' beauty and 'perfect' homes, and inevitably we compare such ideals with what we

have. It is a waste of your potential if you judge your self-worth based upon how you measure up to others. It is far more constructive and healthy to judge for yourself what *you* regard to be important and work towards achieving personal goals to make yourself the person *you* want to be, and not who the media says you should be.

- Even if you are single and worry about time running out to start a family, there are ways in which you can start this process: adoption, fostering, sperm donation, surrogacy and IVF, to name a few.

Just because you are single doesn't mean you can't enjoy yourself! Be more proactive: go out, take an evening class, visit the cinema, book concert tickets, go to the restaurant you've read a great review of, take the holiday you've always wanted to go on. Being single is something that you should enjoy. It's an opportunity for you to focus exclusively upon yourself and do exactly what you choose. It may feel daunting to do such things at first, but with time and experience you'll soon come to realise that it is nothing to be concerned about and you will start to feel much more independent, secure and confident. The more you go out, the more likely it is that you will meet new people, and who knows where that may lead?

17. The dating scene in big cities like London

Our expectations have changed a lot when it comes to meeting a partner. For the first time in history, women are independent – professionally, financially and in their choice of lifestyle.

In big cities, men's expectations are also very high, but in a different way. Men still tend to be attracted to younger and beautiful women who project some vulnerability and who they can protect. At the same time, modern society dictates that men should also look for successful partners who are independent but also willing to enter a relationship, a combination that is not always easy to find.

At Seventy Thirty, we meet hundreds of single people every year who want to find a partner, and we are often struck by a common misunderstanding: men don't seem to realise that, however successful a woman's career may be, she still likes to be swept off her feet. Women still want men to take control in terms of gestures – opening doors, for example, or paying the bill on the first date (even though most women will then reciprocate on the next date). At Seventy Thirty, we have clients aged between 25 and 70, with the majority in their late 30s or 40s, which means that many have come out of long relationships and are not familiar with dating etiquette in the 21st century: for example, if they were in a fifteen-year marriage, there were no emails or texts when they last dated, so there is new etiquette to learn. We encourage people to talk on the phone as much as they can, which is a much better way to express emotions than texts and emails, which should be kept for practical arrangements only.

There seem to be so many single people in London: so many wonderful men and women, and yet so many who can't seem to find someone suitable. In fact, it is much easier to find a partner in a smaller community, which has strong core common values, than in a big city like London, where there is such a variety of peoples of all nationalities, religions, etc. Because there is so much choice, there are many potentially compatible partners for each person, but the problem is that they are often hidden in a huge pool of incompatible people.

One other major problem we have noticed is that men tend to find women in London quite intimidating. The art of seducing a woman is slowly disappearing, because many men no longer dare to flirt. We have introduced people who already knew of each other and found each other attractive, but didn't have a clue how the other person felt! Usually this is because the woman expects to be approached, while the man doesn't dare to make a move for fear of being rejected, which is a shame as this leads to so many missed opportunities.

From the outset, each person should decide what they are looking for in a relationship and know themselves well enough to decide what is right for them. Most people have relationship patterns where they keep making similar mistakes, for example by always going for the same kind of people, despite the fact they are wrong for them. So it is important to understand those patterns and break them.

Also, while physical attraction and similar lifestyles help to find someone who is superficially suitable, what will ultimately keep the relationship together is a common approach to life, for example in terms of attitudes towards money, family or health. Two people can have very different personalities and yet have a very successful relationship as long as they share the same values. Sexual compatibility is also very important: if chemistry is there at the beginning, then it can be maintained and rekindled in the long term. If not, this quickly becomes a major problem.

How do we go about meeting the right partner in big cities like London? It is important to get out there and socialise – the more people you meet, the more likely you are to meet a partner. That may seem obvious but, while many single people do go out a lot, they tend to stay with their friends rather than mingling with people they don't know.

It is also important to promote your image, by making an effort to dress well and look good, which in turn will make you feel good about yourself and therefore more attractive to others. At a time when people are increasingly busy, there is a huge need for professional matchmakers.

Matchmaking agencies like Seventy Thirty can be a great help, as we proactively 'headhunt' for suitable partners and filter out unsuitable ones. Nowadays, people have personal trainers, personal stylists and life coaches to help them in various areas of their lives, so it makes sense to also seek professional advice to find a life partner.

PART THREE: The quintessence of matchmaking

18. The history of matchmaking and its role in today's society

Matchmaking is the art (and business) of bringing people together. Although our contemporary understanding of this notion is usually associated with archaic stereotypes, understanding the history and importance of matchmaking helps you to appreciate the modern-day matchmaker in today's society.

The rituals associated with courtship have always been confined to arranged marriages, with the purpose of procreation. Paying experienced matchmakers for their services for the business of love, wealthy families with youthful, beautiful daughters were usually the predominant market. Matchmaking has been around for thousands of years and is prevalent in almost all traditions. For example, in conservative Jewish communities, the *shadchan* (Hebrew for *matchmaker*) was often involved in the process of *schidduch* (matchmaking), solely with the purpose of bringing together singles within the orthodox Jewish community with similar religious attitudes under the eyes of *Yahweh*, or God.[3] In ancient Japan, matchmakers (or Nakodo[4])

---

[3] http://en.wikipedia.org/wiki/Shidduchim.

were go-betweens for the wealthy, powerful and beautiful. An integral part of the culture, they negotiated all terms of marriage prior to the ceremony, often providing counselling and support to both families throughout the process, since dating was non-existent and marriages were principally business transactions based on enhancing status rather than based on love.

In other societies, the role of matchmaker involves promising one newborn to another according to their celestial compatibility. For example, in traditional Hindu culture, prospective partners are often matched according to the positioning of the sun, the phases of the moon or the alignment of the stars. Affiliation to a matchmaker is often highly sought- after, and in many cases different generations of a family will use the same matchmaker. Today, the role of matchmaker can incorporate everything from relationship therapy and life coaching to teaching seduction.

Another element of modern matchmaking which differs from traditional matchmaking can be understood more effectively using psychologist Abraham Maslow's *hierarchy of needs* (see figure). He explains the key is essentially the motivators that human beings need in order to feel fulfilled. The hierarchy is divided into five segments, or levels, with self-actualisation at the very top of the pyramid; one must satisfy each dimension of the model in order to progress upwards; a core element to succeeding when it comes to personal development. Maslow's stages are seen as a

---

[4] http://japanese.about.com/library/weekly/aa080999.htm.

zeitgeist even by today's standards and are a useful tool to uncover deeper truths about the world of matchmaking and its evolution. Traditional matchmaking dictated a more extrinsic emphasis when it came to the partnering of individuals; everything from our most fundamental physiological needs for human existence and survival, to our need for safety. As mentioned above, the purpose of relationships prior to the turn of the 19th century was to procreate. Despite the common misconception that matchmaking is motivated by the third dimension of *love/belonging*, modern matchmakers, although taking our human need for intimacy strongly into account, go above and beyond these realms. Today, values are the most important facets that connect two individuals. Matchmakers seek to address the higher two tiers of the pyramid as they seek to help people who are highly intelligent, independent and self-aware. Our need for *esteem* is strengthened by matchmakers, increasing confidence, belief in our own achievements and validating self-respect through making us understand what we actually want and what makes us feel good.

Ultimately, the most critical difference in matchmaking historically and its role in today's society is that it fulfils Maslow's highest pinnacle, the need for self-actualisation. In the simplest sense, this means that matchmaking presents something deeper than simply partnering you with a stranger with similar hobbies. Matchmaking provides you with an individual with whom you can be the best version of yourself: someone who ignites your creativity, injects your life with spontaneity, helps you to solve your problems. This motivation is fuelled by our desire to be free from prejudice and content with acceptance of ourselves. Expressing your true self to another without the fear of rejection, and achieving a real, genuine connection, is the focus of matchmaking today and what Seventy Thirty prides itself on.

In a time when online dating produces very mixed results, those who are truly dedicated to finding someone exceptional have once again returned to the precise art and powerful business of matchmaking to fulfil their need to find a life partner. At its core, matchmaking today *gives you control*. It gives you the power to decide who *you* want to be with. In contemporary culture, this highly personalised service, tailored to cater to you, actually delivers on the promises that most other dating mediums fail to do. Purposeful and full of integrity, matchmaking at Seventy Thirty aims to give you a fulfilling experience and memorable journey in your quest to find someone who makes you whole and happy.

19. The rise in people using matchmaking and dating agencies

A number of people I have spoken with recently believe that one of the reasons for the increase in people registering with matchmaking and dating agencies is the growth of global terror organisations witnessed since the start of this century, and which has led to widespread feelings of worry and vulnerability.

Is there any evidence that a relationship might exist between global terrorism and our dating behaviour?

Existentialist philosophers and humanistic psychologists would argue that there is a relationship and that the perception of threat that accompanies real or implied acts of terrorism has psychological consequences on our subsequent behaviour, including our interaction in romantic relationships. This is despite risk perception being a very individual experience, with some people experiencing stronger perceptions of risk than others. When our awareness of our mortality is heightened, by threats to our own and others' existence, this results in existential anxiety: anxiety that is underpinned by uncertainty about our own survival.

So, what happens to us psychologically when we experience existential anxiety, and how might it influence our romantic relationships and dating behaviour?

Psychologist John Bowlby's attachment theory of human development and behaviour (e.g. Bowlby, 1969)[5] suggests that we seek emotional connection and support from significant others, including romantic partners, as an outcome of our existential anxiety. Research by Putnik and Lauri (2004),[6] found that interpersonal relationships tend to

---

[5] Bowlby, J. (1969) *Attachment and Loss. Volume 1: Attachment.* New York: Basic Books.

become closer in the aftermath of a perceived existential threat.

Now to the really interesting point: what happens if we are not in a romantic relationship when our mortality is challenged by a threat? Research by Mikulincer et al. (2003)[7] found that when we experience an increase in awareness of our own mortality, it prompts us to form and/or maintain long-term relationships and, further, that these relationships protect individuals from the effects of existential anxiety. In addition, research by Florian et al. (2002)[8] found that romantic relationships provide individuals with a sense of security.

So, it is not at all unreasonable to suggest that the rise in the use of matchmaking and dating agencies may in some way be linked to existential threats. Matchmaking and introduction agencies provide a stable solution for finding then forming romantic attachments in a world that can seem dominated by uncertainty.

[6] Putnik, K. & Lauri, M.A. (2004) Coping mechanisms and social support during aerial bombing. *Social Psychology Review, 6,* 14–29.
[7] Mikulincer, M., Florian, V. & Hirschberger, G. (2003) The existential function of close relationships: introducing death into the science of love. *Personality and Social Psychology Bulletin, 7,* 20–40.
[8] Florian, V., Mikulincer, M. & Hirschberger, G. (2002) The anxiety-buffering function of close relationships: Evidence that relationship commitment acts as terror management mechanism. *Journal of Personality and Social Psychology, 82,* 527–42.

20. The right measure of love: from addiction to fear of bonding

Psychology has been successful in highlighting the nuances of human connection and how people behave. Our assessment of our own mental health is most closely connected to our sense of success in the emotional and the professional spheres. To paraphrase Freud, if we are achieving our potential, engaging socially and professionally, and at the same time have good and meaningful emotional connections with other people, we feel good, our mental health is good, and we are happy. When we ask how to measure happiness and love, we can say that they are measurable by assessing our professional and emotional goals.

If mental health depends on love, what does love depend on? The answer is simple – on readiness to emotionally bond. An emotional bond is a requirement for a quality relationship. It indicates that some individuals are important to us, that they matter, that we have a sense of belonging and that we treat these individuals in a special way. It is believed that the need for affectionate bonding is a primary, deeply rooted human need. Our first experiences of bonding with important figures (parents) in many ways determine our patterns of connection and bonding in partner relationships at a later stage of life. All people desire to connect, with other people but many do not succeed, due to various fears.

First, there is the fear of intimacy. Individuals are afraid of intimacy have superficial relationships, often based on sex, and they do not allow themselves to open up and share. These behaviour patterns are most often related to the fear that they will be rejected by their partner once they discover 'what kind of person they really are'. At the core of such a fear is the insufficient ability to accept oneself; low self-esteem; and, consequently, a deep sense of unhappiness. Thus, individuals with low self-esteem are likely to refuse or at least be unable to connect with their partner in any meaningful way. These individuals will have had painful experiences of rejection and suffering, caused by significant persons in their life, including former partners. Since they avoid intimacy, they feel lonely and empty and they compensate for feelings of loneliness and insecurity with constant flirting and short-lived sexual encounters. By engaging in such relations, they receive immediate short-term confirmation of their own value ('people don't want to have long-term relationships with me'), which further blocks their ability to connect.

Second, there are individuals for whom partnerships – relationships based on love – are the only purpose of living, and who feel that they do not exist outside this kind of intense relationship. They are able to create connections with significant others quickly and easily, and commit to every relationship. However, they often have difficulty in setting boundaries between themselves and their partners, who are perceived as their only source of security and happiness. This type of bonding is pleasant at the outset of a relationship because they are experiencing intense emotions and feel worthy and empowered. Soon after, however, the partner begins to feel under pressure. Emotionally dependent individuals tend not to show responsibility, but insecurity and low self-esteem.

In relation to both these types, a healthy connection to another person is based on readiness and trust, while being aware of your own and your partner's needs. Healthy connections are coupled with healthy boundaries.

Connecting to another person means allowing that person to get close to you, to reach your inner being, as well as allowing yourself to show intimacy and tenderness. Bonding is a prerequisite for true love and quality relationships.

In assessing their partners, many people rely on 'chemistry' or 'intuition', which are basically unconscious processes that may be based on childish or unrealistic fantasies. While chemistry is important and intuition can play a part, true love includes a realistic and accurate assessment of a partner. For a good relationship, it is important to know yourself: to know what you want from a partner and a relationship, the needs you expect to be met by your partner, and what your *values* are. Values are defined by the reader based on what is important to them; however, generally speaking values are things we believe in. This could be a religion, the importance of family, or having children, or spending time together; it could also mean the importance of your career or attributes such as honesty, intelligence, etc. 'Values' may also mean intrinsic core values

– for example, one person may value loyalty and commitment to a relationship, whereas another might value freedom and the option of practising polygamy!

When we recognise our feelings, we have control over them and we use our feelings as a driving force in the right direction; we build foundations for empathy and developing appropriate relationships. We start loving someone once we have ascertained that they meet our criteria and we are sure that they are becoming important and valuable to us. However, the criteria that we set must be realistic and not standards that are impossible to meet.

Every relationship is a process that undergoes certain phases – attraction, collecting information (partner's personal history, their values, attitudes, goals), assessment (to enter the relationship), and emotional bonding (readiness to get closer to the other and establish a relationship). However, three factors are crucial for establishing a genuine emotional connection: *a balance between giving and receiving, compatibility* and *sincerity*. If we live without love that is based on these values, then we are living in a world that has no emotional value to us.

21. Keeping expectations realistic

Some of us may have one particular unrealistic expectation that relates to who we desire to see ourselves with ('he *must* look like George Clooney' or 'he *must* be more successful in business than I am'). This minimises the pool of potential matches to such an extent that you are likely either to wait a very long time, or never find that special someone at all. It's not possible to predict who you will have chemistry with – so don't be too rigid. Get out there and meet people.

In other situations, it is not so much that one or two of our expectations are completely improbable; rather, we may have so many (relatively rational) expectations that we create a huge shopping list, not realising that there is no shop in the world that could possibly stock all those goods. Being too specific about what you expect leaves little room for anyone to fill the void.

Expectations about the type of relationship you see yourself in can also be problematic. Look out for contradictions in what you think you want, so you don't set yourself up to fail ('he will be totally loving and attentive, yet still remain intriguing and mysterious'). Don't believe that the relationship will always feel as passionate as it does in the first few months; chemistry is a trickster. It's important to separate chemistry from compatibility, and check that you and your partner have enough of both – if you are enamoured with someone it can be easy to feel that nothing else matters. However, in order for a relationship to go the distance it's crucial that there is more involved than just lust: there also needs to be respect and friendship.

And lust does very often fade – scientists have even managed to track this. They believe a hardwired 'love' response evolved because it kept two people together long enough for their offspring to survive (in hunter-gatherer communities, young infants would have needed two parents to survive). They estimate that the honeymoon period lasts for about two years. You should only enter a relationship that is based purely on chemistry if your expectations are aligned: you only want to have fun. However, if you want a fulfilling, long-term relationship, you need to be realistic about the effort needed to maintain the chemistry and think about some of the compatibility factors below.

The right man or woman cannot fix your life or 'complete' you: forget all the rom-coms you have seen, and the façade of happy couples around you. Spend some time making sure you are fulfilled and happy as you are. Only then will you be in a position to meet someone from whom you will not demand too much (and ultimately drive away).

Shedding unhealthy expectations is the first step to gaining a healthy, happy relationship. So what expectations can we keep hold of? Which are the healthy ones?

The first step is making sure you do not confuse unrealistic expectations with high expectations, as this is a common mistake for many people. High expectations do not need to be unrealistic as long as they reflect reality, following a true evaluation of yourself. Intelligent, successful and driven women are compatible with equally intelligent, affluent men.

The second step is to set some boundaries and have a clear idea of what you will not put up with. Start with a little work on yourself: knowing yourself and being honest is a great first step to take. You should never compromise your core values for a relationship.

Identify your core values: start with the tangibles. For example, do you want children? Work out what your views are on marriage, family life, male and female roles, etc. Look at your lifestyle, health and fitness habits (including smoking, drinking and/or using drugs), your energy levels, your interests, your life stage, your religious practices and political beliefs – even your location. Also, ask yourself what kind of relationship would work for you. What if your attachment style? How do you respond to affection? What is your sex drive like?

Most importantly, once you have all this information, stay open-minded. Many people can be compatible with you without sharing all the same interests. So do not fall into the trap of thinking you have to have everything in common (except, of course, major long-term desires such as having children or not). Chemistry is important as well, but understanding the limitations of lust will give you a more realistic view of what genuine love consists of.

22. Investing in yourself

We seem to have no qualms about investing in our friends, family, kids or careers. We will invest in our companies, our employees, our properties and finances, but for some reason investing in ourselves seems to be something we are not so good at. Investing in ourselves is about more than just devoting time and money to our appearance, our wardrobe and our physical fitness and health. The most neglected area of 'us' is usually related to our emotional and psychological wellbeing and self-esteem.

Life coaching is a fantastic platform for people who have not previously invested in their psychological wellbeing in any meaningful or sustained way. Many people are working harder than ever to keep their current job or business alive, but the time this takes leaves other areas of their life wanting. Of course, we only have so many resources as human beings, and to a certain extent some imbalance is inevitable, but those who choose to invest some of that time and energy in themselves and their self-esteem will find dealing with tough times much easier.

We are constantly told to invest in property, in the stock market, in a pension, yet one of the best and long-lasting investments we can ever make is to invest in our self. Regardless of the area of your life you feel needs the most focus, personal development and growth come from goal-setting, actions that help achieve this, and positive thinking.

Not only are our values the reasons behind our life choices; in any relationship, shared values are the key to longevity. Yet many of us do not even know what some of our most fundamental values are. To understand more about your core values, try the following exercise.

Rate how important to you each of the below are on a scale of 1-3 (1 being extremely important):

- Health
- Appearance
- Friendship
- Social life
- A variety of interests and activities
- Marriage
- Having children
- A stable relationship
- A passionate relationship
- Ability to devote time to family/children
- Freedom and independence
- A fulfilling career
- A financially comfortable life
- Independence
- Creativity
- Freedom to create, change and choose my own lifestyle
- House ownership
- Spirituality and religion
- To contribute to my community or to charity – the greater good

- To be remembered for my accomplishments
- Helping those in distress
- Abundance of leisure time
- A stable life
- Solitude
- Roots in the place I live

Now, take a look at each of those you have rated as being 'extremely important'. These are the things you will never be fully satisfied without. By acting in accordance with your values, you will start to attract people with a similar mindset. You and your partner do not have to share all the same values, or share the same timeframe (for example, your partner may also want kids, but they may want to focus on another area of life first) but it is very important that a future partner has similar values to you, so you can live together and be happy.

It is not uncommon to both crave and fear affection at the same time. This disorganised attachment pattern is shown by people who want to achieve a real emotional closeness with a partner, but fear opening up and getting too close to someone who then has the power to reject them. In this situation, relationships often do not work because one of the people in the relationship has needs that cannot be fulfilled. For example, they crave closeness but select someone who is unable to provide this; someone who is cold or emotionally unavailable.

23. Four ways to improve your image

What should you wear on a first date?

We all know how important first impressions are: within seconds, your date will have formed an opinion of you. Rather than putting too much unrealistic pressure on yourself to look flawless, choose an outfit that you feel both confident and comfortable in, while knowing you've made an effort. You're confident because you look good, are dressed appropriately for the occasion, with good shoes, you have great personal hygiene and your hair looks good. You are comfortable because you have not gone over the top, you're not fidgeting with your outfit and you feel like 'you' – your outfit reflects your personality.

Of course, make sure that you have taken practicalities into account, such as location, time of day, crowd and activity. Remember, if you want to be taken seriously and are looking for a long-term, committed relationship, don't over-expose yourself: too much too soon in a relationship can create instability and it often ends as quickly as it starts. Take a second to appreciate yourself. Faking anything (other than your height in those sexy heels you're going to be wearing) is pointless, so the best advice, as clichéd as it may sound, is to be you – the best version of yourself.

Is image as important as personality?

To answer this question, let's think about how a relationship starts. We meet someone to whom we are 'attracted' in some way; we have great chemistry with them; we build a connection; that connection becomes a bond; the chemistry become less explosive and more stable as the bond is cemented. Image plays a very important role in igniting the fire for most people; it may not be as important as personality, but it is the gateway. We initially assess an image to give us clues to someone's deeper character, and what this person will be like in the long term. Image may also be important, in the long term, to keep that flame burning. Our image is a reflection of our personality and values (among other things, such as status). A change in our image suggests changes in other factors, and could raise alarm in a relationship. Image is very powerful. It should not be confused with 'looks'; it's how we present ourselves. We should not compare image to personality; we should combine them, because that's sexy! At the same time, don't let your intrinsic self be overshadowed by your extrinsic self, because nothing is more alluring than a genuinely charming and charismatic character.

How do you use psychology to understand what attracts an individual to another?
The physical elements of attraction are actually only a small part of one's overall attractiveness and (as mentioned earlier), what men find attractive can be different to what women find attractive. In addition to how we present ourselves, much of a man's attractiveness comes from his charisma, confidence, aura of power/success, charm (and how he makes others around him feel), manners, the way he holds himself, walks and talks. Much of a woman's

attractiveness comes from her femininity, her general and emotional intelligence, her positive attitude and warmth.

We are all very different in terms of what we find attractive and, often, what we look for physically is a clue to the qualities we seek in a mate.

How do people go wrong with their image?

By social comparison: we may evaluate ourselves based on other similar people around us; this may be upwards or downwards. Downward comparison helps us gain self-regard while upward comparison reduces self-regard, which we probably do more often to make us strive to be better. When it comes to our image, there is a huge amount of social comparison taking place, otherwise how would we know how to present ourselves appropriately? However, this system may fail sometimes because one can't just copy what works for someone else.

Sometimes people get their image wrong because they are trying too hard, and attempt to follow what is on trend rather than dressing for their body type and personality. If you are uncomfortable in a dress, you probably look it. It is also true that sometimes there is a disconnect between how we see ourselves and how others see us. Some people struggle to put together an outfit; they take everything out of their wardrobe, finally settling on an outfit they hope looks good. Then again, some people claim not to care. Not conforming to what's in fashion is a statement of individuality.

24. You can only gain as much as you put in

Business-savvy men and women tend to invest in finding love and a relationship using the same energy, creativity and passion that led to their career success. Seeking a partner should be viewed as an investment in your life, and should be approached using many of the same principles you apply to other major life decisions, such as finding the right job or the right home. When seeking a partner, we subconsciously rate ourselves on desirability factors such as physical attractiveness, intellect, social status, wealth, youthfulness and health. People with high levels of self-awareness and self-esteem are more likely to rate themselves accurately and therefore have a realistic view of true compatibility.

Once you have found a truly equal partnership (and remember this is not solely a question of looks, which may not come into the equation at all, but equals in terms of humour, outlook, values, hopes, dreams and beliefs), the next stage is investing in the relationship. Psychologists have recognised a parallel between economics and relationships: relationships work on an exchange of costs and benefits, similar to the marketplace. A relationship will be successful if both partners perceive that the rewards, costs and contributions to the relationship are equal on both sides. As Eric Fromm, the German psychologist and philosopher, once said: 'Love is often nothing but a favourable exchange between two people who get the most of what they can expect, considering their value on the personality market.'

However, problems can occur when people take these kinds of business principles too far and expect to invest a minimum amount for the maximum return. Relationships, unfortunately, don't work like that – you can only gain as much as you put in (there is no such thing as a bargain!). People who have high levels of self-awareness are more likely to assess the balance of investment and reward from both sides of the relationship and maintain equilibrium. If you approach relationships intelligently and with the same passion, creativity, spontaneity, time and effort that you apply at work, then the rewards for both partners can be wonderful.

PART FOUR: Money and relationships

25. Money and romantic attraction: do only men stand to benefit?

One of the major indicators of success in modern society is money. Western culture often places an inordinate emphasis on the power of money and material wealth; this can be seen in today's 'celebrity' culture and the constant bombardment of media advertisements for the next 'must have' item.

Some women are led to believe from a young age (through societal norms and values) that men should be the 'provider' within a relationship; this can lead to entrenched core values about male and female roles in a relationship. Therefore, these women may seek a man to be sole provider, as this allows them to play the traditional female role within a relationship, even when they are successful and financially independent in their own right.

However, most people, when looking for a long-term relationship, prefer intelligent partners who have a good sense of humour, are friendly and have a great personality, as this helps to build an equal, cooperative relationship. This is mirrored in our experience of matchmaking at Seventy Thirty; we have found that there are commonalities in what successful men and women look for – and they are certainly looking for more than just a pretty face when considering a suitable partner for a long-term committed relationship.

26. Why is money such a big issue in relationships?

Money is a big issue in every aspect of our lives – not just within relationships. We need money to feed ourselves, clothe ourselves, express ourselves, enjoy ourselves, develop ourselves and challenge ourselves. Money talks, and it says a lot about us; it therefore has an overwhelming impact on our self-esteem, self-confidence, self-belief and feelings of self-worth.

If finances are a problem, then an individual will understandably feel concerned, stressed and anxious, which will affect their relationship. A major problem can be comparing oneself with one's peers and being left feeling inadequate and unsuccessful.

In dating, it's normal to want to treat your partner and spoil them, to show your affection for them, but if the means by which you can do this are restricted, it can sometimes feel as if your ability to show your affection is lessened.

Within a relationship, the traditional dynamic of 'man as breadwinner, woman as homemaker' can be traced back to our evolutionary history when hunter-gatherer males provided for nurturing, maternal females and their children. By providing well for their female partners, men guaranteed the increased health and success of their offspring, which in turn increased the likelihood that their genes would be passed on to the next generation. This adaptive behaviour shaped the minds of modern humans; therefore we are still inclined today (no matter how subconsciously) to follow this path.

Understanding our evolutionary history makes it easier to see why relationships involving a powerful and financially successful woman may be problematic. Being with a woman who earns more than he does can impact upon a man's sense of masculine identity (thus making him feel less secure), and it also influences a woman's sense of feminine identity (thus making her less 'dependent' on her male partner). Both these scenarios bode badly for a relationship.

Of course, there are many examples of successful relationships in which the woman is the main breadwinner. A major contributory factor in such successful relationships is trust: when two people are honest, open with and trust one another, any insecurities about money, success or power are dispelled and these couples can enjoy a very secure, content and fulfilling life together.

27. Power struggles

Even with the best intentions, many couples fail to achieve a successful power balance in their relationship. Psychologists believe that a power imbalance is driven by three main factors: social norms, psychological dependency and inequity between personal resources.

Power cut

When one partner is seen as powerful, the other may feel they have to submit to them, particularly if they are financially or emotionally dependent. Feeling powerless can lead to resentment, which is often expressed passive aggressively, such as through withdrawing emotionally. A relationship can be poisoned by the feelings of loneliness that accompany powerlessness, since loneliness can result in the partner seeking attention elsewhere.

However, a healthy power dynamic can be created when an equal power balance is striven for. It means valuing your partner's attributes and recognising each other's strengths. Remember, being with another person is a choice, so when times are difficult focus on what attracted you to each other in the first place. Power dynamics are also not static. They are fluid, often dependent on external factors, and may very well change throughout a relationship.

Power in love

When power is equally shared in a relationship, communication is more likely to be direct and effective, which means both partners will feel valued and respected. It is a virtuous cycle that results in a continuation of the shared power balance. This allows both partners to maintain their own identity alongside their shared identity as a couple. A couple that practises equal power sharing will be able to deal with conflict and stress more easily. Remember: when power in love is shared, your relationship is likely to be more powerful.

28. The gold-digger

There is nothing wrong with being attracted to a successful man or woman if this is because they have qualities such as drive and ambition that you find appealing. For gold-diggers, however, this is the sole reason for starting a relationship.

The key common features among gold-diggers include the fact that many have a troubled background and that they are usually quite materialistic (sometimes to the extent that this represents the sum total of their identity). This can be a dangerous combination.

Many gold-diggers have experienced betrayal, neglect or hurt in their childhood. As a defence mechanism to protect them from future anguish, they do not want to be reliant on someone for love and intimacy again. They maintain detachment between their emotions and their actions. Sex and love are not one and the same thing for gold-diggers; instead, they are easily separated. This means it is a lot easier for sex to be perceived as a commodity. Thus a gold-digger is not usually someone who wants to meet a partner for love, emotional support, intimacy or companionship, but rather someone who is driven by monetary rewards.

Modern society emphasises the importance of wealth and often creates the illusion that all one needs to be happy in life is money. Insecure people who compare their lives with those of celebrities are very susceptible to these messages, and may conclude that money is all they need in order to feel fulfilled, happy and content. Gold-diggers fall into this category, and tend to look for a quick fix, with a focus on temporary but tangible rewards. This alleviates their feelings of dissatisfaction and emptiness in the same way that alcohol or drugs do for others. But of course when the effects wear off, a gaping hole is left that still needs to be filled, and so the cycle continues.

But surely those who partner with gold-diggers have a role to play in encouraging (even if subconsciously) this negative and destructive behaviour? Many wealthy people have worked very hard for their financial success. Those at risk of attracting gold-diggers tend to be those who have neglected their emotional state of mind at the expense of that success.

If someone is unfulfilled in one aspect of their life, yet successful in other areas, they may use the area in which they are successful to fill the gaps in other areas. So a rich man or woman who is insecure about their attractiveness, perhaps whose partner has recently left them, or who is worried about getting older may unconsciously use their plentiful resource (in this case, money) to balance the situation out. Thus they choose to buy attention, companionship and admiration. Of course, you cannot really buy these things, but you can buy the illusion of them: in the short term, this may work well but it is highly unlikely to yield any long-term gains for either party.

You may ask if this kind of relationship can ever be positive for either partner. This depends on how much the person's financial status has played a role in the development of the relationship and also whether there is any genuine mutual attraction and compatibility. In some cases, genuine feelings can allow each partner to grow emotionally and change their behaviour. However, this tends to be the exception rather than the norm.

In the longer term, these kinds of unhealthy relationships can exaggerate people's original issues and insecurities. A relationship that is created from mutual need will only encourage a lack of trust between partners; each will constantly worry that their partner will get a better offer. This will only heighten each party's insecurities, which in turn can lead to controlling behaviour, power struggles, increased likelihood of affairs, and loneliness and depression.

This type of relationship may feel positive in the short term; however, such a superficial partnership means that neither party will be truly fulfilled, which is the hallmark of a genuine loving relationship.

PART FIVE: Dilemmas of love

29. Are you sabotaging your chances of finding long-term love?

You know that you want to have a long-term relationship, but it just never seems to work out. Either your relationships last no longer than a few dates or a few months, or you are finding it hard to meet someone at all. If this sounds like you, don't despair. Often, people will unconsciously block their own path to love and happiness. To make sure you have the best chance at achieving your desires, ask yourself the following questions:

Do I feel that love will just happen rather than choosing to work for it, as I would for success in other areas of life?

Love does sometimes happen with a glance across a crowded room. But this is only one way it can happen. Many of us will never accidentally bump into the right person, as is often shown in romantic films. Love is an area in which we never have full control, but that does not mean we should leave it all up to chance.

Do I lack balance in my life?

Life has a habit of getting in the way of love. If you are overly focused on your job, your family, or other problems and challenges, it can take most of your time and, of course, you will have less time to think about – less alone focus on – love and finding the right partner. Sometimes other areas of life need to take priority, but sometimes a focus on work is a shield against being vulnerable and putting yourself out there. Be careful that you don't raise your guard too high; protecting yourself too much makes it difficult to let someone else in.

Am I missing opportunities?

While you don't want to get into a relationship that is not right for you, it's important that you keep an open mind and take the time to get to know someone. Sometimes, the right person may come in an unexpected package. Be sure that you aren't focusing on aspects that are unimportant (e.g. the car they drive or the way they dress). Your expectations should be focused on core factors that are fundamentally important to you, including personal qualities, values, beliefs and lifestyle.

Am I too impatient?

Being single and seeking a perfect partner, someone whom you know is right, can certainly be challenging. It may take some time; it may take joining different groups and getting involved in a wide variety of activities. Some people may meet the person who's right for them in a supermarket or at work. For others, it may take much longer. But remember, however long it takes makes no difference once you find it. The love you feel will be the same wonderful, powerful force whether it takes a day, a year or a decade to find.

Do I mistrust my intuition?

Second-guessing or ignoring our instincts is rarely a positive thing. Trust yourself! Fear and self-doubt are traps that can sabotage your chances of finding love. They also give other people the power to convince us of something we may feel is not right. Listen to what your gut tells you, and if you meet the person who makes everything feel as though it fits just right, do not ignore it. It's hard to let down your guard, which protects you from rejection and hurt, but the only way to find love is to open your heart fully.

30. Love hurts

One interesting study carried out recently by researchers at the University of Michigan found that when participants were subjected to the sight of an ex-lover who had broken up with them, they showed the same brain activity as when they were subjected to extremely hot stimulation on their forearms. Emotional and physical pain have more in common than just making us feel bad; they share sensory brain regions, too.

Many (although not all) types of physical pain will have a set healing process and an end date. Most extreme emotional pain, however, does not. We may revisit an episode of unresolved emotional pain years, if not decades, after the event that caused it, and find we still have strong feelings of distress. We cannot, however, remember having a broken ankle, for example, and induce the same sensation. Emotional wounds simply do not heal in the same way as many physical wounds do.

31. Why do men lie?

The way we think and act today has been shaped by the thoughts and actions of our ancestors. In order to be successful in evolutionary terms, an individual had to survive and then transmit their genes into the gene pool of the next generation; since the only way in which we can achieve this is through sexual reproduction, we are all inherently predisposed to reproduce.

It is therefore clear that, to be evolutionarily successful, one should have the desire to produce a number of healthy offspring.

A major difference between men and women, however, is the 'investment' required in producing offspring. Theoretically, a man can impregnate many women in one day and not have a burden of responsibility, whereas a woman, once pregnant, must carry and nurture this child for nine months (a massively consuming task in terms of time and energy expenditure), and then is also considered the natural caregiver, thanks to her ability to breastfeed. Regardless of the desire to have children or the joy in having them, it is undeniably more costly for a woman to reproduce than it is for a man. This inherent imbalance means that, biologically, women tend to seek out partners who will be good-quality mates in terms of parenthood as well as in terms of marriage, whereas men are biologically inclined to seek a high number of mates.

However, if *both* parents take responsibility for a child, the child is likely to be stronger, more intelligent and healthier, and will therefore be more likely to successfully reproduce, thus ensuring that the genes of both parents are carried forward. Over centuries this has resulted in men and women acquiring the ability to form strong emotional bonds with one another as this benefits their child, thus improving the child's (and therefore both parents') evolutionary success.

Psychologically, we are predisposed to believe and trust others; if we are told something that sounds plausible (and we have no cause for suspicion), we generally accept it to be true, especially if what we're hearing is what we want to hear, as this satisfies our ego!

32. New relationship know-how

No one has the perfect relationship all the time. Couples often take each other for granted, give ultimatums, try to change each other and hold the unreasonable expectation that the other is responsible for making them happy.

Part of building a strong, trusting relationship is starting off on the right foot. Here are seven common mistakes we make in new relationships and what we can do to stop them from happening.

1. *Getting rid of excess baggage*

We all have a dating/relationship history. While it may be tempting to share our life story with a new partner, certain subjects, such as ex-boyfriends/girlfriends, should be left on the carousel at the baggage claim terminal. Each new relationship offers the chance for a fresh start, but we spoil this opportunity when we reintroduce old injuries back into our life. If you still can't stop thinking about your ex, then this is a sign that you are not ready to be in a new relationship.

2. *The ex projection factor*

Just because an ex cheated on you doesn't mean that every other partner will too. It's a good idea to resist the temptation to project your ex's faults onto a new love interest. Unjustified mistrust only creates further mistrust, damaging the relationship from the outset, making it difficult to develop intimacy. If you find you're attracting the same type of partner, none of whom is making you happy, it's time to rethink your dating criteria.

3. *Being too picky*

Some people who find themselves in new relationships on a regular basis do so because they have very unrealistic expectations. There is a big difference between core values and preferences. Holding out for honesty, integrity and a strong character are all worthwhile qualities, but 'must keep DVDs in alphabetical order' is not.

4. *Making a mountain out of a molehill*

We are often suspicious of new relationships because we don't know the person very well. It's very easy to make a mountain out of a molehill, especially if your last relationship was characterised by mistrust. But try to remember that people make mistakes. Your partner will, and so will you. Before you jump to conclusions, take a step back. It's rarely worth sweating the small stuff. For instance, if your partner is running a little late for a date, it doesn't mean they deserve the cold shoulder or that they have done this to inconvenience you. Keep perspective on what's important.

5. *Creating special time*

Remember, a date is about getting to know someone. Keep your phone out of sight. The world has become so obsessed by keeping in touch that many of us have forgotten how to enjoy the intimacy (and romance) of a one-on-one conversation.

6. *Obsessing*

Try not to read too much into the things that happen during each date. Don't cling to each word, trying to work out what your partner is thinking, don't obsess about the look on their face when you used the word 'we', and don't constantly look for signs that indicate how the date is going.

Sometimes, by adjusting our actions because of what we *think* is going on, we can ruin a good thing that would have been better off if we'd just let things take a more natural course.

7. *Ignoring red flags (or warning signs)*

If your love interest is obviously not in tune with your most important values, pay attention to your instincts. So if they become narcissistic (excessively selfish, uncaring of others), treat people rudely and are increasingly critical of you, it's likely time to move on before leaving becomes more difficult.

33. Men approaching women

How we set out on our search for a partner to love and to receive love from occupies a great deal of time – for both men and woman.

Searching for a partner and taking the initiative by making the first move takes time and a *lot* of thinking. When a man approaches a woman, his ego is at stake. Men associate feelings of worthiness with their ego, and if they encounter a situation where their ego may be reduced or challenged, they feel unworthy and ultimately unmanly. So what is it like to make an approach? Well, some men would say that making an approach is like an interview from hell. 'What if she doesn't like me?', 'Have I read the signals well enough?' and 'How do I introduce myself?' are but some of the fears that a man considers before he can take that step forward. Studies have shown that many men will take the 'safer' option and approach a woman who may not be his physical ideal, but who he thinks is less likely to reject him.

In some situations, the dynamics of approaching a woman become so overwhelming that it is essential to have a 'nothing to lose' frame of mind. Wanting to know about the woman who is in front of you will play far more in your favour than using hackneyed chat-up lines (which only work if you have something damn good to back them up). If you do approach a woman in this way, your mindset will naturally be that there is nothing to lose as you will have no expectations.

Beauty – and attraction – are in the eye of the beholder. I firmly believe we create attraction regardless of our looks, even in a world focused on surface beauty. I assure you that the men who are most successful with women are average-looking guys who have nothing to lose and would like to meet a fantastic lady. Their attitude has placed them one step closer; they are more focused on meeting someone than on their ego.

Making yourself known and remembered is also vital. We all differ in our own special ways; simply find out what separates you from everyone else and what makes you the individual that you are, and make this aspect of yourself attractive.

On this basis, men should remember two key factors: 'be different in an attractive way' and 'your enemies are insecurity and neediness'.

So, how should women handle being approached? We all love compliments and sometimes men may try too hard to impress; they may watch too many movies and be influenced by them, so, ladies, please do bear with them. Once over the first-approach jitters (highly prized egos are at stake, remember), they are actually really great guys.

Awareness of the non-verbal language of attraction also plays a role here: the rule of four. This means that if one shows a minimum of four non-verbal attraction signals to a man, he will subconsciously assume we are attracted to him. Being aware of the signals that we are giving off may prevent someone from, or entice someone into, making an approach. A momentary exchange of glances opens a non-verbal dialogue, which is loaded with sexual potential. If you re-establish eye contact, you have already given two signals. Other signals indicating that we want someone to come closer could include leaning towards the gentleman, for example, or an even simpler gesture such as a tilt of the head or a smile. So, ladies, be aware of the signals you are giving off!

Ladies, if your glances are mistakenly interpreted as a come-on, and you are faced with a gentleman in whom you are not interested, everyone appreciates politeness: a simple 'no, thank you' is always refreshing. Perhaps you could combine this with changing your body language so that the message is clear, but not insulting.

But a word to the wise: never judge a book by its cover. You might be surprised, or even intrigued, by what he's got to say. As you know, beauty is but skin deep and beauty is in the eye of the beholder. This is more often than not true and, who knows, you might actually learn a few things about yourself and meet an interesting person if you take the time to do so. Once you have mastered body language, you can listen to him without leading him on.

Men, ask yourselves: what is my motivation for the approach? If a woman is approached, she should ask herself what she would like to gain from the chance encounter. This is a wonderful position to be in, as we may meet an incredible person who can introduce a new dimension to our lives!

34. Is kissing another person cheating?

A kiss is the ultimate expression of affection, romance and, of course, love. If you are tired of hearing the excuse of 'it was just a kiss!', let's explore what just a kiss actually means.

Evolutionary psychologists define the importance of kissing as 'mate assessment'. According to a study conducted by Hughes, Harrison and Gallup,[9] a kiss is used to determine

---

[9] Hughes, S.M., Harrison, M.A. & Gallup, G.G. (2007) Sex differences in romantic kissing among college students: An evolutionary perspective.

whether a particular person is worthy of being future partner material.

The best kissers are more likely to be chosen as life partners. Kissing behaviour dictates that a passionate kiss arouses sensations of arousal, leading to expressive feelings of bonding and attachment. Therefore, on an evolutionary, physical, sexual and emotional level, kissing is a deeply meaningful act.

35. Do confessions make relationships stronger?

As human beings, we are naturally curious. We are all drawn to, and curious about, other couples' confessions and secrets. At Southbank's Love Festival in London, a wall of confessions allows us an insight into what naughtiness others have been involved in: a married woman's recent lesbian experience with her oldest friend; a man's confession that he is still in love with his ex-wife after being divorced for 21 years; a woman's admission that she secretly meets her partner's brother while he out is at football. We read each handwritten note while we tightly hold our own partner's hand, thankful that our relationships are so stable and honest.

But are they? With up to 60% of married individuals committing adultery,[10] a confession may seem a perfect way to free you of your sins. But when it comes to confessions in a relationship, is honesty the best policy? And, if so, will it make your relationship stronger?

First, the two building blocks that form the foundations of a relationship are *truth* and *trust*, and they are cemented together by communication. No matter what the nature of the confession, remember: relationships cannot work without honesty. Lies, even little white lies, can be a catalyst for other problems, creating an unstable and unhappy relationship.

Take, for example, confessing a sexual desire; you may have a fantasy or sexual interest that you want to explore with your partner but just can't seem to tell them about it. This could be an act that is important to your sexual happiness but you feel too embarrassed or even guilty to mention it. This is perfectly normal, but it's important that couples are completely honest if a relationship is to work in the long term. Not telling the truth about your desires, and a lack of openness, can push couples apart and can lead to one individual looking elsewhere for the experiences they crave. As long what you desire is between two consenting adults, it is better to discuss it than to bottle it up. Your partner may be uncomfortable with your fantasy; if so, this is something that you can discuss together, but they may also have fantasies they have been too embarrassed to mention to

---

[10] http://www.truthaboutdeception.com/cheating-and-infidelity/stats-about-infidelity.html.

you. Communication is key in any relationship. It helps couples to move forward – thus making them stronger.

Take also, for example, a confession of cheating. It goes without saying that cheating is not appropriate in any loving relationship, and to confess to cheating may seem like a sure-fire way to ruin your relationship and your partner's trust in you. This may be the case. However, it is not healthy to live with any kind of deceit in a relationship – for either the cheater or the cheated. Now consider speaking with your partner about why you cheated – this may open up a discussion about other important issues in the relationship. Do you both feel fulfilled? Appreciated? Loved? Is there a deeper problem that, because of a lack of truth and honesty, has not been discussed?

Cheating is the end result of a larger problem. If you can discuss that larger problem, you can begin to create a stronger, more successful relationship. Seventy Thirty psychologists agree that if the individual who cheated confesses, admits they were wrong and is honestly remorseful, it can allow *trust* to be rebuilt and *truth* and honesty to begin to be restored.

For good psychological health, confession leads to a sense of relief, forgiveness and understanding, known as the curative effect. It allows us to disclose information about our thoughts, feelings and events which, in turn, leads to better psychological and even physical health.[11] Experimental

---

[11] http://experimentaltheology.blogspot.co.uk/2008/05/postsecret-part-4-postsecret.html.

disclosure experiments have identified that confessions –
even confessions not disclosed to another person but
written down – allow you to experience and externalise your
emotions, creating a better sense of self. Good self-
awareness can subsequently improve your participation in
your relationship and result in a stronger relationship.

In order to truly love, you need to be open to, and risk,
being hurt. A confession may break your relationship, but
often – for your own conscience and own mental health – it
may be necessary. If you can confess your deepest desires
and needs, a confession can strengthen your relationship
and make it more successful in the future.

36. Moving from friends to lovers

Many of the most-envied relationships are ones with a
strong friendship at their core – the partners can trust, talk
to and count on each other. Indeed, evolutionary
psychology suggests that women prefer a strong
relationship to be built up before romance develops.
However, certain courting rituals are evident across all
cultures. An example of this is a man making displays of
acceptable aggression, for example taking the lead, making
the first move (not waiting for the woman to do this). A
woman's genes are trained to respond positively to this type
of behaviour, as it is linked to a man being able to offer
protection to her and any future offspring.

- Is there a specific time frame from meeting a woman to going in for the first kiss?

One of the main differences between friendship and a relationship is sex – so you must allow your friend to see you in a sexual way. You can't act like a friend with a woman and expect her to become attracted to you. Instead, you must begin *acting* like a lover before she can begin considering you as a lover. This does not mean being lecherous; rather, it means being bold and forthright – again, an aspect of the courting ritual. You should be upfront and honest about your intentions, so that not too much time passes without a woman you are interested in entertaining the thought of you as more than just a great friend. There is no textbook answer dictating the timescale from meeting a woman to the first kiss. It is about using your interpersonal skills to detect verbal and non-verbal cues from your partner and finding the moment when she wants you to kiss her!

Most of this delicate communication is done through body language, and the right time will be when you simultaneously start mirroring each other's behaviour, i.e. you will make eye contact for longer and start making more physical contact. Catch her unawares and she'll think you can't control your hormones – a clear sign of immaturity. Leave her waiting too long, and she may start to look elsewhere.

- How can you make your intentions clear from the start? What traps do men fall into (being too nice, etc.)?

There are also typical 'friendship behaviours' that should be avoided when attempting to move from friend to lover. Don't allow her to talk about other guys she's interested in – always change the subject from this type of conversation. Create a bit of distance between you – don't always be available, don't always be her shoulder to cry on, keep some masculinity and mystery about you so that she wonders where you are and who you're with. Don't just spend time with her – organise something special for the two of you to do. Take control and be spontaneous – impress her. Also, don't forget to flirt – subtly. Tell her she looks great; compliment her; offer to cook dinner – be irresistible.

Various non-verbal cues can be used and picked up on here too – if you were to be a little more flirtatious (hold her gaze for a little longer, be more complimentary about her), after a while she should start to give off some signals. Maybe she will look deep into your eyes for longer than normal, maybe she will make subtle hints (that you probably won't notice unless you are watching for them so do be aware). Alternatively, she might just come straight out and say she is interested in you.

37. Love at work

A lack of romance and love can affect one's life and emotional wellbeing. Love is a fundamental human need, and loving others allows us to put the needs and desires of others before our own. Those of us with fulfilled needs are well-rounded, happier and generally more productive.

Today, there are more than 13 million single people in the UK. While many relish the time and space to focus on themselves, some are unhappy: perhaps they feel lonely, or they work long hours and have limited time to socialise and embark on new hobbies. This is a common fear; many people worry about meeting suitable partners, especially when they have little time for investing in new friendships and activities.

In big cities, meeting someone special can feel difficult, especially if you don't belong to any groups or do any activities outside work. It can be easier to find a partner in a smaller and close-knit community. However, this does not mean you must pack your bags and head to the nearest village; it means connecting with people who share similar interests and activities. In fact, the bigger the city, the more likely it is that you will meet like-minded individuals.

You just need to know where to look. If you like history, join a local history society. If you like running, there are many running groups that put as much emphasis on fun and socialising as they do on running. If you like music, familiarise yourself with the local music scene – find out where local bands play. Think of the activities *you* like to do and what things you feel passionate about, and then go and look for like-minded groups or activities and get involved.

38. The summer fling

During the summer, it's not just the sun that sizzles. Pulses start racing as people peel off the layers and emerge from winter hibernation. A phenomenon begins that resembles something seen in a nature documentary. Men and women congregate on beaches or in bars and pair off at a rate that would make your head spin. Passionate affairs continue throughout the summer then, as the days start to cool down, so do these short-lived romances.

So, what exactly is happening and how wise is it to seek summer love?

Scantily clad bodies, mood and social influence all play a part in summer romances. As we all know, physical attraction is a key element of finding a partner, especially when you are only seeking a short-term blast of passion. During the summer, when people are showing much more flesh than usual, hormone levels are boosted. Women also feel much more attractive in the sun, which alters body language dramatically, giving more sexual signals to men, who in turn pay women a lot more attention. You also may become so accustomed to wearing a skimpy bikini on the beach that when you put on a summer dress in the evening, you feel much more confident than if you were to wear the same dress during winter months – and it's a proven fact that confidence is incredibly attractive to men.

Having a positive outlook on life is another of the most attractive traits that both men and women are looking for. Summer is the happiest time of year for most people, partly induced by the chemical effects of the sun itself. So, as people are smiling and enjoying life, they are more attractive (and more attracted) to others.

Whether you are on the terrace of the Hotel de Paris in Monaco or lazing on the beach, one thing is for sure – people love hanging out with their friends. Everyone feels younger, more sociable and more carefree. The summer is the best time to embrace being single, as many more social interactions occur.

A summer fling is exciting, energising and spontaneous, so it's natural to seek this form of encounter, and there are strong social influences thanks to friends, television programmes, magazine articles and, of course, steamy summer novels.

So, are summer flings wise? If you want one and have one, how can you make it work for you?

Anyone who has a summer fling should do so in the knowledge that they are usually only short-term fun, so don't expect to find a partner for the long term. There are many forms of love, which have varying degrees of three vital ingredients: intimacy, passion and commitment. In a summer romance you may feel very close to your partner and the sex may be fantastic, but this form of romantic love misses out commitment completely.

If you are seeking a long-term partner, then it's best to keep this relationship goal separate from finding a summer romance, as a long-term relationship requires commitment as well as intimacy and passion. That's not to say that summer flings never develop into something more serious: I introduced a couple last summer who first met while they were at their respective villas in Nice. They had a fantastic summer together, but I knew from profiling them that they also had long-term potential as they have similar lifestyles and values. They are now in a very happy relationship and are living together in the UK.

Whether you are just seeking a bit of fun, or ultimately looking for a life partner, there is no harm in having a summer fling if you have realistic expectations from the outset. Every relationship brings its own rewards (e.g. fun and great sex) and costs (e.g. arguments), so taking a few preventative measures can ensure you have a fantastic time without any emotional consequences.

Taking the following steps can help you to be your own relationship expert and get the most from your summer.

1.   Keep your independence – don't ditch your friends or change your lifestyle radically to spend every waking second with your summer love. You can easily make space for him without sacrificing anything else in your lifestyle – remember, your friends will be there for you come rain or shine.

2.   Plan your lifestyle for autumn – maybe this is the time of the year when you decide to focus on something new, such as learning a new language or a new winter sport.

3.   Love yourself more than he loves you – believe in yourself and do not base your self-esteem solely on the attention he gives you. This will help prevent your sense of self-worth from dropping once the romance draws to a close.

4.   Think – you need to be smart and rational. Remember, great sex and good chemistry do not necessarily lead to long-term commitment.

If that sounds too much to handle, then there's always an alternative – avoid summer flings by focusing on other things you enjoy doing during the summer: travel, sports, socialising. Enjoy being single: there are many more ways to have a fabulous summer than having a man by your side.

39. Why do I pick the wrong partners?

We can learn a lot about ourselves from past relationships. With the right mindset, there is no such thing as failure. So you may not have met the perfect partner this time, but you have probably learned something valuable along the way that will help you next time. A positive thinker will take the time to assess, in as fair a way possible, what went wrong and how they can prevent the same thing happening again. But how can you be fair when you're angry, jealous and upset about a break-up? Try to remember that a good partnership is about compatibility between two people. It's not about who was right and who was wrong.

If you are being honest, can you say you supported each other to be happy and allowed each other to grow, no matter how the relationship ended? It is important to be aware that there is a lot that we can do within ourselves to ensure that we seek the right person, that we attract the right partner and that, when we are in a relationship, we act in a way that is healthy

40. Mystery

It has been said that a little mystery can be good for a relationship. It may be true that disclosing deep secrets is a great way to build intimacy in a close relationship, but this works best when secrets are divulged gradually, over time. When a date is going well, a woman may be tempted to share a lot of information about herself. However, try to not overwhelm each other with too much information during the introductory stages of a relationship. This is not to say that you should be coy or secretive – being open, approachable and communicative is always the best approach.

41. Let go of the Prince/Princess Charming syndrome

We are conditioned to believe that we need to find one 'perfect' person who will meet all of our needs for the rest of our lives. The problem that many people have in terms of meeting suitable partners is that they confuse 'perfect for them' with 'perfect'.

There is no such thing as a perfect person – none of us are, and expecting partners to be perfect will only result in disappointment.

Stop looking for the perfect person to fulfil your every need, and instead be open with people with whom you are compatible and share chemistry, and who in fact may be perfect *for you*.

PART SIX: DIY relationship/date coaching

42. How Seventy Thirty's relationship/date coaching works

Libby is a 25-year-old graduate who had moved to London to work as an events manager. Her conversation with friends generally consisted of discussing the latest episode of *EastEnders*, which she proudly recited in a broad Cockney accent (Libby is Scottish). She is a sweet woman and means well but, when we asked her about her knowledge of current affairs, she excitedly responded with her insider knowledge of David Beckham's latest off-the-field antics. But Libby had a fascinating hidden side; she was captivated by art and culture, and enjoyed visiting local art galleries. Intelligent, witty, fun and naturally beautiful, she was a perfect example of a wife in the making.

We used a tailored six-month coaching programme to transform Libby into an articulate woman who could engage in meaningful conversation over supper with her partner and his associates. She gradually progressed from reading *OK!* magazine to *The Times* and, while she was never going to engage in deep political debate, she began to become more interested in environmental issues and world poverty.

Libby was a particularly fun person to coach. After finding out about her ideal man, we enlisted the help of some of our male clients and sent Libby on some dates: one with a gentleman whom we knew was Libby's type and another with a gentleman whom we knew was definitely not. Henry is 38, attractive, articulate, driven and wealthy. Jeremy is 48 (over her upper age limit), extremely wealthy, but rather shy and quiet.

Libby thought the date with Henry was 'out of this world'. The date with Jeremy, she said, was a 'total nightmare'.

The point of the exercise was to video-record the feedback that both men gave after the date to show Libby. Henry said she was an attractive girl but that 'other than that there is not much to her'. He noted that, while he might class her as someone whom he would take on a date, he would be highly unlikely to take her out to meet his friends, family or business associates. Henry said that Libby's view of the world was blinkered and that she was holding herself back and restricting herself. Although he was polite, his message was that Libby came across as a dumb blonde. In contrast, Jeremy (whom Libby didn't enjoy dating), almost drooled over Libby when giving feedback ('She is really hot, she has an amazing figure. Yes, I would love to spend more time with her and take her out on my yacht. In fact, I think we would get on very well indeed – I know my friends would think I was a very lucky man.') When we asked Jeremy to elaborate, he became quite crude and Libby was repulsed. It was apparent that he wouldn't care if Libby couldn't even speak the same language as he did; he liked her body.

There really is no better way to show someone that they are attracting the wrong type of men for the wrong reasons.

After coming to this realisation, Libby was very open to change.

Alyssa is an attractive, sporty, intelligent and ambitious 29-year-old. However, she found it hard to connect with a partner since she lacked confidence in herself. Successful men see a beautiful woman who is not giving off any 'I am single, come and chat to me' signals, so they assume she is already in a relationship and avoid her.

We used a video camera to record Alyssa's behaviour in bars and at social events, to show her how her body language was giving off negative signals to men. We also showed her video footage of some of our experts at work in a bar, so she could see how it could be done. Many women would benefit from having a better understanding of body language – Alyssa definitely did.

Research shows that women initiate around 90% of flirtatious encounters. We worked with Alyssa to explain the importance of eye contact, smiling, preening, body position, speech and touch. More importantly, we worked with Alyssa to get the signals just right. Too subtle and many men won't catch on; too exaggerated and you could come across as desperate. For example, did you know that, when you make eye contact with a man, you need to hold his gaze for exactly five seconds before you look away, and also that (on average) a woman needs to repeat this three times before a man unconsciously accepts that he may approach her?

As well as looking at Alyssa's body language, we refocused her mindset to simultaneously alter her behaviour and thoughts. Once the changes in body language began to pay off it was easier for Alyssa to feel irresistible, which increased her self-esteem, creating a virtuous cycle. Alyssa is now gliding into some of the country's most exclusive venues, setting her sights on men she feels she will have a connection with, and approaching them with confidence, sophistication and grace.

43. How to improve your chances of finding the right person

Finding Mr or Miss Right is rarely an easy task. Most of us have to go through quite a few failed relationships before finally finding the right person.

Don't be afraid to tell people that you are looking for a relationship. But don't focus on superficial traits – for women, try and stay away from 'tall, dark and handsome' or, for men, 'blonde and buxom' – and prioritise what is important to you. This doesn't mean you should ignore physical attraction altogether, as there will need to be some chemistry to attract you in the first place, but placing a strict limit on lust or a person's physical traits will only lessen your chances of happiness. As the Rolling Stones famously said: 'You can't always get what you want, but if you try, sometimes you find you get what you need.' But for this to work, you need to be open to meeting real people, with quirks and flaws like we all have, rather than focusing on daydreams of the perfect person.

If your family, friends and colleagues don't know about your search for a long-term relationship, they can't help you. It's normal to feel a little defensive about being single, but don't let others perceive you as not wanting to be in a relationship. Tell your family, friends and your co-workers: they might know just the person for you. Be open to all possibilities, as the right person could come from anywhere. Don't forget, while you are looking for someone, someone is also looking for you!

The importance of confidence can't be emphasised enough. No matter how tall, slim, or intelligent we are, people are drawn to those who are project confidence. We've said it before: confidence is sexy! If you feel a little unsure, try modelling your outlook and behaviour on someone you admire. Think of a person who is approachable and friendly, and watch the way they interact with others, until this feels like something you could do. Remember, you are not trying to be someone you are not; you are simply helping your personality to shine.

It's also important to remember that if there are issues that you need to work on, such as assertiveness, sharing your feelings, anxiety or depression, finding a partner is not the solution. Take some time to be with yourself and to grow first. It might be useful to seek therapeutic or coaching support. Sometimes emotional difficulties can be a barrier that prevents people from connecting and finding love.

Not everyone is drop-dead gorgeous, but this should not make any difference to how attractive you feel. Very few people look like models in magazines. Most of us are average-looking. However, this is what makes us unique. Not being a model doesn't mean you are not as attractive as people who are more physically perfect. Beauty is in the eye of the beholder, and many things that you may find perfect about a model or celebrity others may not agree with. Women may feel that a skinny six-foot model is the pinnacle of perfection, but many men may prefer women who are short and curvy. Men may think that height, perfect abs and a washboard stomach are what all women desire, but many women will prefer men who are artistic, or funny, or intelligent, regardless of how tall they are or how muscly their chest is. Focus on the things that you find attractive about yourself. If you feel a little unconfident, try writing down things that would make you feel more attractive. It doesn't do any good to fret about body issues: either accept them as part of what makes you unique or, if something is bothering you that you can change, empower yourself to do something about it.

If you feel as if you could do with a makeover, try joining a gym, get a new hairstyle and buy a new wardrobe. Be proud of you!

Meeting the right person could happen anywhere – nightclubs aren't the only place where singles meet, and you don't need to be tipsy to approach somebody. You may end up meeting a potential partner at work, the library, a health club, cafe or charitable organisations. And, of course, a great place to meet the right person is through a matchmaking or dating agency, such as Seventy Thirty. Use your hobbies and other passions to find love. Don't decline an invitation to a friend's wedding just because you happen to be single. Weddings are very good places to meet people.

Be confident and try to meet a wide range of people: you might soon find yourself chatting away to your future lover.

44. Are negative feelings about yourself getting in the way of your feelings about your partner?

If you are feeling low about yourself, you might have negative thoughts, such as, 'My partner does not love me enough.'

People with high self-esteem, on the other hand, are likely to focus on the positive aspects of themselves and their partner. By doing so, they are more likely to project positivity on the relationship, generating a higher sense of commitment from both partners and increasing their overall wellbeing.

Changing the way that you see things will also affect how others see you, causing a virtuous cycle rather than the destructive one you may be stuck in now. For example, thinking, 'No one likes me' or 'I'm not attractive enough' will result in negative, closed-off body language that will stop people wanting to approach you. Thinking, 'I am attractive' and, 'I have lots of good qualities' and smiling will do the opposite.

45. Psychological and physiological changes after a break-up, and how to move on

Breaking up with a partner is tough for both people. It's no wonder that many of us put it off, by remaining in an unhappy relationship, returning to the same unhappy relationship soon after breaking up, or repeating the same issues in the next relationship.

The emotional journey after a break-up has been likened to the grief process. First come shock and denial, then pain and guilt. This gives way to anger and bargaining, followed by depression, loneliness and reflection. Things then start to look up and the pain subsides, at least a little. The final step is about learning to accept the situation and seeing hope for the future.

The process is hard, but it can result in positive changes and personal growth. After a break-up, not only are we in the process of grieving the loss of the relationship, but often we are also coming to terms with a change in lifestyle. Change can be very unsettling, as it means venturing into unknown territory, but if you think of change as positive it is more likely to *be* positive.

It is likely that the longer the relationship lasted, the more there will be to deal with after it ends, in terms of practicalities such as housing, splitting financial resources – and possibly changing schools, if you have children. Financially, the changes that occur after a break-up or divorce can be difficult to adjust to. Relationships with ex-partners regarding child-rearing can become strained. Almost all elements of a person's life will be disrupted during a break-up, bringing about a considerable amount of uncertainty with regard to the future. However, by surrounding yourself with a good support system these major life changes can be a great opportunity for positive change. If you have been dependent on a spouse or partner, use the chance to sort out your finances and make sure you really understand your income and outgoings. Move somewhere you have always wanted to live. Have a house sale, sell unwanted items on eBay or donate items to a good cause. Use the time you would have spent with your partner doing something you are passionate about. Once you have grieved for the loss of your relationship, think of yourself as having a fresh start; a new beginning to your life.

Many psychologists have conducted studies on people who have entered romantic relationships, and what occurs when a relationship breaks down. The studies found that, when people enter a relationship, their lives becomes intertwined, which means that different areas of their lives, e.g. interests and friendships, overlap. Therefore when the relationship comes to an end, many people experience a change in their sense of self: suddenly you are defined solely by your own identity, rather than as part of a couple.

Psychologists have reported that experiences of severe emotional distress activate the same neural pathways in the brain as physical pain does, making some people feel as though they have been hit in the chest. The psychological pain experienced due to heartbreak can manifest itself in several ways, from insomnia to a loss of appetite. Bearing in mind the physical and emotional consequences associated with heartbreak, it is important to try and overcome this pain in a healthy and productive way. Below you will find some tips, which the team at Seventy Thirty have devised.

1. First and foremost, remember that it is totally normal to feel this way. It is not unusual to feel down, angry or hurt, among many other emotions. Don't bottle up your feelings: speak about how you feel to those you trust, and don't be afraid to cry. Crying is the body's natural stress reliever. When we cry, stress hormones that have built up over time are removed from our body – so give in to your emotions and let them out.

2. While you may feel like forgetting your troubles with a glass of wine or two, try to avoid drugs and excess alcohol. This is not a healthy way to get over a break-up. While they may temporarily help to ease the pain you are experiencing, what goes up must come down. Alcohol and drugs will only cover up your problems, not help to solve them, and in the worst-case scenario could

result in you developing a dependency on them when faced with stressful events later in life.

3. Exercise is a great way to get you out of the house and meet new people in a healthy environment. Joining various sports clubs can help you to develop a new sense of self, as you will be making new friends who do not associate you with your previous partner; they are part of your new beginning. Studies have also found that regular exercise can improve your mood and self-esteem, as well as reduce depression.

4. The stress-relieving properties of music have been well documented. Soothing music – such as classical music – has been found to lower blood pressure and heart rate, and reduce the level of stress hormones in the body. Singing and listening to upbeat music has also been found to make people happy, because our brain releases feel-good hormones that lift our mood when we hear it.

5. A good support network is key; don't be afraid to speak to your friends and family about how you feel. Many people worry that other people will get tired of hearing about their problems, so they shut them out. Try to imagine how you would feel if you found a good friend was suffering in silence – you would most likely want to help. The same applies to them. So talk, be open to your emotions, socialise (even when you find it hard) and find constructive ways to give you natural highs.

Remember, a break-up is a normal part of life, and you will come out the other end.

46. The first approach and creating a good first impression

How we set about searching for a partner to love occupies a great deal of time for both men and woman.

Searching for a partner and taking the initiative by making the first move takes courage. Ego is almost always at stake in dating, whether it is yours, in terms of approaching someone, or theirs, when they approach you. So what is it like to approach someone with a view to getting to know them better? Common fears include: 'What if he/she doesn't like me?', 'Have I read the signals well enough?', and 'How do I introduce myself?'

Remember, attraction is in the eye of the beholder. People are attractive for a wide variety of reasons, and attractive to different people. We all differ in our own special ways; simply find what separates you from everyone else and what makes you unique, and focus on this aspect of yourself.

So, how should you handle being approached? Well, remember that it's hard to approach someone you don't know. Treat the person who approaches you with the same respect you would expect to receive if you nervously approached someone – even if you are not interested in getting to know him or her better. And remember, sometimes first impressions are wrong. Although the person may not initially fit your ideal in terms of beauty, handsomeness or height, they may in fact be your soul mate in terms of humour, love and intelligence. Get to know someone before writing them off, and keep your own limitations and flaws in perspective. No one is perfect, not even you.

Awareness of the non-verbal language of attraction also plays a role here. Most important is the rule of four, as mentioned in Section 33. However, never judge a book by its cover. You might be surprised, or even intrigued, by what the person has to say. Think of dating as an exciting time in your life; it means you have the opportunity to meet an incredible person – if not a potential partner, then possibly a future friend.

Here are some tips on how to appear more attractive when creating a first impression:

- *Non-verbal behaviour is key* – as discussed earlier, non-verbal behaviour makes up about 70% of our communication. Therefore, it's not necessarily what you say, it's how you say it that is important. Make sure that you smile, make eye contact and be aware of your tone of voice, as all of these factors will go a long way in creating a good first impression.
- *Pay attention* – people tend to be attracted to others whom they feel will be attracted to them, so pay

attention to the people around you. If you want to catch the eye of someone you find attractive, then make sure you look their way.

- *Don't be afraid to let your intelligence shine through* – intelligence is an attractive quality and it also makes you stand out from the crowd.
- *Be natural* – don't feel that you have to hide behind a mask: just be yourself. Show your personality.
- *Be confident* – if you are secure in yourself then you are more likely to attract the right kind of person. This will also help to improve the flow of conversation, increase levels of humour and will also help you to appear enthusiastic and full of life.

47. Seventy Thirty's rules on a first date

1. *Build up your confidence.* Dating can be nerve-wracking even for the most confident person, and we all have a tendency to visualise the worst-case scenario on a date. Before you go out, do a healthy 'asset inventory': make a list of all your good qualities. Picture yourself being relaxed, confident, at ease and enjoying a wonderful date.

2. *Dress the part.* Do your research and find out about where your date is taking you and plan your outfit accordingly. Classic rules of clothing etiquette should apply. Look your best but don't wear anything uncomfortable; you'll wind up focused on how your clothes feel, rather than your date.

3. *Watch your body language.* Posture and eye contact can send messages that speak louder than words. Get to know yourself and visualise how you want to connect with your date. (Our Seventy-Thirty members are often coached on their body language ... millionaires or not, it's an often-neglected area of focus.)

4. *It's not therapy; it's a date.* Don't talk about nightmare exes, bad dates you've suffered, or horrible primary school stories. Keep it personal, but positive.

5. *Don't talk money.* Discussing finances on a first date is a big no-no. You're there to get to know each other, not your bank accounts.

6. *Don't drink too much.* It is a tempting option to calm your nerves by throwing back martinis, but this will only make you more likely to stumble into regrettable choices.

7. *Skip the sex (at least at first).* So you're hitting it off and the person across from you has your heart pounding. Great! It might sound old-fashioned, but resist the temptation to give in to your primal urges before you've got to know the person better. Saving something for later will keep both of you wanting more, and will enable you to connect on a deeper level.

8. *Have fun!* While you can't guarantee every date will be a success, you *can* increase your chances of this by being as relaxed and positive as possible on your date. And dating is supposed to be fun, remember?

48. Your best possible self

Sometimes it's good to check in on where you are now, where you would like to be and how you plan on getting there. The vehicle to success is you, and only *you* can make sure that you are your best possible self. Take some time to visualise your best possible self five years from now. Try and imagine the most detail possible: where will you be living? What kind of job will you be doing? What sort of activities will you be involved in? Will you have children?

- Try writing about your future self. This will help create a logical structure for the future and can turn your abstract ideas into concrete possibilities. Note the strengths of your future self and any changes you will need to make now in order to turn your vision into reality.
- Take a few minutes every day to remind yourself of this vision, keep it fresh in your mind and remember that you can achieve it if you want to.

When things go wrong – we all have bad days – it's easy to become focused on the negative and lose direction and motivation. Visualising your best possible self can help to re-establish your priorities in life.

As you imagine your goals in life, you will also find ways to overcome obstacles. Today can be the start of a new chapter in your life. Focusing on the positive things to come, and putting the past behind you, can be very therapeutic.

49. The importance of meaningful goals in a relationship

Once you move past the initial attraction stage, setting meaningful goals in a relationship can help to ensure that you are on the same page as a couple – and it also helps to keep the relationship vibrant rather than static. There is also more likelihood that the relationship will succeed over the long term if a couple has shared values and their individual, relationship and long-term goals are complementary. Goal-setting not only helps to outline what each person wants from the relationship; it also means the support of another person who understands you and what you are trying to achieve. Outlining goals can help couples understand what's important to them both, and creates intimacy in the relationship as it encourages open and transparent communication.

To ensure that you are a good fit with your chosen partner, listed below are some of the things to think about when approaching love in this way.

- What are your short-term goals?
- What are your long-term goals?
- Where do you see yourself in six months? A year? Ten years?
- Which areas of your life are you willing to make compromises in?

-   Which aspects of yourself are you not willing to change? Why? (This will help you enter a relationship with a better sense of your own identity and what you most value about yourself.)
-   Do you want marriage or children?

Once you have defined realistic goals, then you can work as a couple to put the steps in place to make the relationship work. Where there are differences in your visions, you may need to work together, communicate and look at ways that you can both compromise. Make time to reassess your individual and relationship goals, as these can change over time, and you need to make sure that both people in the relationship feel that their needs are continuing to be met.

Though it is important to understand your partner's goals, you also have to take into account your needs. Taking a more pragmatic approach to love and having more realistic expectations of relationships can actually be an empowering process. This doesn't mean that chemistry, lust and attraction are not important – it's about making sure you have the best chance at love. When a person addresses their own needs, this tends to increase their self-esteem and confidence. Therefore, if you approach love in this way you are more likely to meet people who will be compatible with you, as well as increasing the success of your relationship working out.

50. Self-esteem

We develop self-esteem though positive life experiences: as young children, through our relationships with family members and teachers; at school, through academic achievements and social inclusion. We compare ourselves to others and assess our worth. Receiving positive reinforcement when we have done something well, or for being funny, intelligent or good looking, can help boost self-esteem. However, not doing well, and feeling unpopular or being bullied, can lower self-esteem.

People with healthy self-esteem tend to have firm beliefs and values, but are open to different views and secure enough to adapt their position.

Our self-esteem can come from the satisfaction of doing something well. When you are feeling low about yourself, it might be because there is something you could be doing better. Rather than sinking into depression, acknowledge your feelings and allow them to motivate you to focus on improving whatever it is you feel low about. Healthy self-esteem is vital in order to attract the kind of people who will be good for us.

51. How to stay on top

Every day, take a few moments for yourself!

What to do each day

Monitor your thoughts – don't let yourself talk negatively. Your unconscious mind is always paying attention to what you say. Even if you are soothing yourself by saying, 'I don't need to feel nervous about that presentation' you are heightening your awareness to the fact that you're feeling nervous in the first place. So think as positively as you can. Try saying to yourself instead, 'This presentation will be a good learning experience.' It works much better. Leave self-deprecation to other people – being negative about yourself may make others laugh, but it's not the best approach in terms of strengthening self-confidence.

What to do each week

Make sure you find some time to visualise exactly what you want out of life. You may be dreaming of a promotion, or about losing a few pounds, achieving a sporting goal, rekindling a lacklustre relationship, or something else entirely. Spend time visualising your goal and watch yourself living that goal on a movie screen inside your head (as though it has already happened). By doing this you will become more familiar and aligned with what you seek. Research has shown that the more we identify with our goals, and the more detail we give them, the more likely we are to achieve them in the long term.

What to do each month

Reward yourself – everyone responds well to rewards! However, rewarding yourself haphazardly, while it may be fun, does not work. Think about when you should treat yourself. Reward yourself only when you have done something positive towards your goal or tried very hard at something. Be honest with yourself and give yourself genuine positive encouragement as you strive towards your goals. Be sure to find a reward that works for you – if dieting, avoid food as a reward and perhaps buy yourself a new book, DVD or piece of jewellery instead. Rewards are essential, and even a small reward, such as saying something nice to yourself, works – it costs nothing and makes you feel good.

What to do each year

Review old goals and set new ones – goal-setting is great when we set goals that we genuinely want: goals that are realistic, positive and meaningful and where we completely understand our motivation for wanting them to begin with. Setting meaningful goals is something everyone should do regularly. Why? Because goals focus our attention and direct our efforts (and when tied in with a reward, research shows that we become much more persistent, too). However, it is important to set realistic goals that are achievable. So instead of saying, 'I am never going to eat cake again!', a better goal would be, 'I am going to allow myself dessert twice a week.' The goal should be within your control – a goal that will not lead to failure and to you eventually giving up and wrongly attributing the failure to yourself.

52. Valentine's Day

Buying gifts for your valentine depends on what you're trying to achieve. In life we either give loved ones situational gifts (birthdays) or tactical gifts ('I really like you'). In many animal species, males give tactical gifts to females to woo them, and females have evolved to expect tactical gifts as a display of commitment or intention. What some men fail to understand is that women want to see you being tactical on Valentine's Day; in fact, they expect it.

A standard card from a shop with your signature in will mean little more than no card at all. It's about showing you care and investing something precious (time and brain power, in this instance) into maintaining or creating the relationship.

And if the thought of writing something profound makes you dizzy, or if you can't spell, we suggest drawing a picture. Women are drawn to intelligent men.

Don't use the commercialisation of Valentine's Day as a cop-out. Sometimes the simplest gesture can increase the attraction. Find out what your valentine likes to eat, and cook her favourite meal for her. Or forget the food: scatter romantic candles around the house and offer your valentine a massage instead.

53. Ten tips on what to look out for when forming a relationship, and how to keep it

1. *Don't confuse lust with love.* During the initial stages of a relationship, many of us are guilty of confusing those fiery feelings for love. Try not to rush into any commitments too quickly, as later down the line you may find that those feelings you were experiencing were lust, nothing more. Love has to be based on more than attraction and chemistry.

2. *What are their values?* Before entering a new relationship, ensure you take the time to establish what is most important to your partner. What are their values in life? And, most importantly, what do they expect in a relationship? At Seventy Thirty we have found that when relationships come to an end this is often due to differences in values and relationship goals.

3. *Turn a positive into a negative.* When forming a romantic relationship, think about your past relationships and why they did not work out. Was there anything you could have done differently that may have saved the relationship? If so, and if it is relevant to your new relationship, make sure to apply these changes, to give you and your new partner the best chance of success.

4. *Let them know they are on your mind.* For many people, the road to success is not an easy one, often requiring high levels of dedication and long hours in the office. If you leave for work before your partner, send them a text at around

the time their alarm goes off. This will make your partner feel more loved and remind them that, although you are not with them, they are never far from your mind.

5. *Remind them that you care.* After some time in a relationship it's normal to feel comfortable, but it can be easy to take your partner for granted. Unfortunately, this is never good for relationships. In order to give your relationship the greatest chance of success, make sure you regularly remind your partner how deeply you care for them. This can be done in a variety of ways, from a compliment, to holding their hand or even a kiss on the forehead. Little gestures like these tell them how much you care, and can be much more effective than one night of passion every few weeks.

6. *Accept your partner for who they are.* You cannot enter a relationship with someone and expect them to change to fit your lifestyle. If you are from very different backgrounds, learn about your partner's background, whether a different culture, religion or class. Additionally, learn to accept not only what you love about your partner, but those habits that you may not be so fond of. Remember, there are probably things that *you* do that they do not like. Don't highlight their shortcomings – this will only lead to negative feelings towards you and insecurity on their part, both of which can damage a relationship.

7. *Remember, a relationship is a two-way street.* Show respect to your partner and treat them in the way that you wish to be treated. Having a mutual level of respect for one

another will encourage you to think about your partner's feelings, and to acknowledge them as being as important as your own, even if you do not agree with the way they feel sometimes. It also teaches you not to set unrealistic standards for them, e.g. completing tasks that you would not be willing to do yourself.

8. *Make time for each other.* Maintaining a family and a career can be difficult but, irrespective of how busy your life may be, make sure you make time for your partner. While you may not have time to go on a date, try to set aside an hour before bed when you can talk to one another and share your thoughts, feelings and any worries. Be supportive of your partner if they are going through a tough time at work or facing other difficulties. Remember, even if you cannot provide practical help, emotional support is just as important. This can be something as little as a hug and reassuring them that everything will be OK.

9. *Tell them how you feel.* It's good to want to show your partner how much you care, but sometimes it is better to tell them. We all appreciate a romantic gesture, but don't forget to talk to each other as well. The moment you stop communicating with your partner is when you begin to distance yourself from them. Maintain a close connection by talking to your partner.

10. *Maintain a sense of self-respect and identity.* While we all want to be the best partner we can be, this does not mean condoning or tolerating any form of abuse directed at you (or your children). Any abuse – whether it is physical or

emotional – is a clear sign that you should end the relationship and seek professional support.

54. The perils of relationships at Christmas

The joy (and success) of Christmas is largely dependent on how you approach it. It's OK for children to focus on wanting lots of presents, a holiday from school, and to receive lots of attention, but for adults this is somewhat selfish and counterproductive. Many couples can fall into a negative spiral at Christmas. Psychologists generally agree that just after Christmas is the most common time of year for people to seek some form of help with a relationship. The main hazard couples must all learn to avoid is heightened or unrealistic expectations about an 'idyllic' Christmas day, or a 'perfect' Christmas present from a partner. Most of us expect, from a very young age, Christmas to be the time of year when everything is perfect. The problem is that life is not idyllic. It's full of surprises and inherently changeable. Yet, despite our experience teaching us to the contrary, many of us, perhaps for this very reason, cling to our expectations around Christmas and the romanticism attached to it.

However, rather than feeling disappointed, we need to be aware that when we all have such different ideas of constitutes perfection, not everyone will be pleased with the same things. It will never be 100% perfect every year, but if you manage everyone's expectations the result can be a wonderful Christmas break.

A lot of resentment can arise between romantic partners at Christmas and other holiday seasons, with one person feeling that they have put in more effort than the other. Remember to balance things out: talk things through with your partner and plan in advance which of you has the time to do what. With regard to presents, don't tell your partner that you 'don't want anything special this year' and would rather they be 'more practical with money', unless you truly mean it. Another cause of tension is surprises: if you surprise your partner with an expensive gift and they haven't reciprocated to the same extent, they are likely to feel guilty, alongside resentment. Try to keep lines of communication open to ensure you are both aware of each other's hopes and desires.

55. Expert tips to make the most of the festivities

Here are our ten exclusive tips on how to best to manage the stress of Christmas.

1.   Accept that this time of the year is stressful. Our expectations are in direct proportion to the amount of stress we experience during the holidays.

2.   It's important to remember is that perfection isn't necessary to create priceless memories. Focus on the special

(and sometimes silly) moments that everyone will remember.

3.   Being mindful, focusing on one thing at a time, staying in the moment: all help to slow you down and decrease stress. One trick when you are feeling stressed during holiday-related activities is to look at your feet, notice where they are and focus your energy on that place for a moment, grounding yourself in the present.

4.   During the holidays, it may seem as if there are an infinite number of additional activities to pack into our already hectic schedules. You may have to go to some events, but there are others you can say no to. Take the time to check in mentally, think about each event and its importance to you, your family and your friendships.

5.   If you are separated or divorced, the holiday season can be upsetting, especially if your children are spending time with your ex. Rather than being hard on yourself, if you're feeling angry or lonely, try to accept your feelings. For many people life actually takes a turn for the better once they accept the divorce. Make up your mind that you're going to keep the drama out of your children's lives; allow Christmas to be a joyful time for them.

6.   Delegate: most women are wonderful at multi-tasking. Share the shopping, cooking and cleaning with your partner: you don't have to do it all yourself! Remember to enjoy the company of your loved ones. They have come to see you, not your perfect, clean house.

7.   Avoid overeating or drinking. When the brain gets stressed it sends out signals for you to eat fat and sugar, which is why the holiday season can be so bad for our waistlines. The best way is to plan indulgences and have a healthy morning-after plan.

8.   We make lists and strategies for many areas of our lives. This year, make a 'holiday success list' of the things that are most important to you.

9.   Taking care of yourself during this hectic time is essential, in order to maintain a sense of balance in your work and home life.

10.   This is a time of year to help others, to focus on those less fortunate than ourselves and to be grateful for the good things in our lives. Take a deep breath, relax and have a happy, healthy holiday.

PART SEVEN: Everyday psychology, exclusive tips

56. Be your own psychologist

Most people can benefit in some way by applying psychology to different situations in their lives. The good news is that you don't need to be a psychologist to benefit from it – anyone can use it. Psychology can help you better understand your family and friendships, work, relationships and feelings around intimacy. Here are just a few tips on how you can benefit from using psychology in your everyday life.

Deal with sensitive people more effectively

Many people are sensitive – maybe you have colleagues, friends or family who are sensitive. Such people feel things more acutely and react quickly and deeply to situations. This can be difficult for both themselves and others, so what can you do to understand and communicate with sensitive people better? When working with a sensitive person, you should avoid using negative language. Rather than saying, 'Don't worry', try changing it to, 'Stay calm, everything is under control.' This is because the use of negative words can lead too-sensitive people to feeling more upset. Did you know that, when we hear a sentence, we process the word we hear last? For example, if I were to ask you not to think about a white bear, what do you find yourself thinking about? A white bear, of course! When telling someone, 'Don't worry,' the first word they will process is 'worry', and the word 'don't' will come last, when the worrying has already kicked in.

Identify stressors and how to cope with them

While small doses of stress can be good for us, long-term stress can be harmful and lead to ill-health. The main stressors in life are those we feel we have little or no control over. Psychologists have observed that people who feel a problem is out of their hands are likely to have a more intense emotional and physiological reaction to it. When faced with situations where we feel we are losing control, the best option is to adopt an appropriate, result-focused, coping strategy. For example, you may be experiencing problems in introducing your children to your new partner and feel your children's emotional reaction will be out of your hands. A way to overcome this would be to take a proactive approach. Seek advice from people who have been in similar situations, and ask how they handled it. If you do not know anyone who has been in this situation, speak to an expert or friend, or try easing your children in to the new situation. Ask your children how they would feel about meeting him or her, and tell your children as much about your partner as possible before introducing them. Also, make sure that you spend plenty of time with your children, so they do not feel that your new partner is taking you away from them. Unfortunately, we cannot always take control of every situation; for example, the death of a loved one. The most we can do is find ways to cope with our emotions.

When faced with a difficult situation, it is helpful to surround yourself with family and friends and a good support network – even if you do not want to talk about what has happened, having someone nearby can be a source of comfort.

Maximise your support network

Have you ever wondered why people are often so protective of their family? Even when relationships between family members are strained, during difficult times family members usually come together to help and protect each other any way they can. According to evolutionary psychologists, we are protective of family members (in many instances regardless of the situation) because kin selection enables us to look after a common gene pool. This has been used to explain a variety of altruistic behaviours and also to explain why a high percentage of friendships break down as a result of one party disliking the other's family or family members (such as their children). Capitalise on the natural support network of your family who, in many instances, are already motivated to look after your best interests.

Find a fulfilling relationship

Choosing to commit to a lifelong partner can be difficult. Evolutionary psychologists have suggested that, when selecting partners, men and women look for different qualities than they possess, to ensure a more balanced relationship. However, we are more than just biological vehicles for our genes. Understanding psychology helps us to understand the broader picture – background, value systems, relationship goals and lifestyle goals are just as important as chemistry in terms of longevity in a relationship.

57. Making it work – relationship rules

• *Choose your partner wisely*. We are attracted to people for all kinds of reasons. They may remind us of someone from our past. They may shower us with gifts and make us feel important. Evaluate a potential partner as you would a friend: look at their character, personality, values, their generosity of spirit, the relationship between their words and actions, their relationships with others and how they treat other people.

• *Don't confuse sex with love*. Especially at the start of a relationship, attraction and taking pleasure in sex are often mistaken for love.

• *Know your needs and speak up for them clearly*. A good relationship is not a guessing game. Many people, men as well as women, are afraid to state their needs and, as a result, camouflage them. The result is disappointment at not getting what they want and anger at their partner for not having met their (unstated) needs. Closeness cannot occur without honesty. Your partner is not a mind reader.

• *Respect, respect, respect.* Inside and outside the relationship, mutual respect is essential in a good relationship.

• *View yourselves as a team.* This means you are two unique individuals bringing different perspectives and strengths. Remember, the value of a team is in combining your differences in a positive way.

• K*now how to manage differences.* This is a key aspect of success in a relationship. Disagreements don't sink relationships. Name-calling and being uncommunicative do. Learn how to handle the negative feelings that are the unavoidable by-product of the differences between two people. Stonewalling or avoiding conflicts is *not* managing them. Everyone fights at some point, even the best-suited couples. Arguments can be a healthy part of any relationship as long as you and your partner understand how to communicate and work out any issues in a calm manner as adults.

• *Communicate.* If you don't understand or like something your partner is doing, ask about it and why they are doing it. Talk and discuss: don't assume.

• *Solve problems as they arise.* Don't let resentments simmer. Most of what goes wrong in relationships can be traced back to hurt feelings, leading partners to erect defences against one another and to become strangers or, even worse, enemies.

• *Learn to negotiate*. Modern relationships no longer rely on roles dictated by strict social norms. Because people's needs are fluid and change over time, and life's demands change too, good relationships are negotiated and renegotiated all the time.

• *Listen*. Truly listen to your partner's concerns and complaints, without judging them or him. Much of the time, just having someone listen is all we need to solve problems; it opens the door to confiding worries and fears, which is at the root of real trust.

• *Be empathetic*. Empathy is crucial for a long-lasting, solid relationship. Remember to look at things from your partner's perspective as well as your own.

• *Work hard at maintaining closeness*. Closeness doesn't happen by itself. In its absence, people drift apart and can be susceptible to affairs. A good relationship isn't an end goal; it's a lifelong process maintained through regular attention, communication, trust and respect.

• *Take a long-range view*. A marriage is an agreement to spend a future together. Talk about your dreams regularly to make sure you're both on the same path. Update your dreams every so often.

• *Never underestimate the power of good grooming.*

• *Sex is good, but pillow talk is better.* Sex is easy; intimacy is difficult. It requires honesty, openness, self-disclosure, confiding concerns and fears, as well as hopes and dreams.

• *Never go to sleep angry.* Say sorry to one another. Say 'I love you'. Be kind to one another.

• *Apologise.* Anyone can make a mistake. Being able to say sorry is crucial, and highly predictive of marital happiness. Attempts to apologise can be clumsy or funny, even sarcastic – but the willingness to make up after an argument is central to every happy marriage.

• *Forgiveness.* The flip side of an apology is forgiveness. If your partner apologises, don't reject it. Accept it fully and put the fight behind you. Don't bring it up again in future disagreements.

• *Maintain some independence.* Some dependency is good, but depending on a partner for all your needs is an invitation to unhappiness for both partners.

• *Maintain self-respect and self-esteem.* It's easier for someone to like you and to be around you when you like yourself. Meaningful work – paid or volunteer – is one of the most important ways to exercise and fortify a sense of self.

• *Keep things new.* Enrich your relationship by bringing into it new interests from outside. The more passions in life that you have and share, the richer your relationship will be. It is unrealistic to expect one person to meet all your needs in life.

• *Cooperate*. Share responsibilities. Relationships only work when they are a two-way street – with equal give and take.

• *Stay open to spontaneity*.

• *Maintain your energy. Stay healthy.*

• *Recognise that some times will be better than others.* Recognise that all relationships have their ups and downs. Working together through the hard times will make your relationship stronger.

• *Be self-aware.* Make sense of a bad relationship by exploring what went wrong. Don't just run away from a bad relationship; you'll only repeat it with the next partner. Use it as a mirror to look at yourself, to understand what you are doing to help create this kind of unhealthy relationship.

• *Love isn't static.* Love is not an absolute static commodity that you're either in of or out of. It's a feeling that ebbs and flows depending on how you treat each other. If you learn new ways to interact, feelings can come flowing back, often stronger than before.

58. Healthy, balanced relationships

Turn myth into reality and only attract healthy, happy relationships into your lives.

Attracting a relationship that is fulfilling, based on attraction, mutually loving, fun and exciting – while at the same time yet free of any problems – is perceived by many as a myth ('you can't have it all'). Yet, finding this kind of relationship occupies the thoughts of most single men and women. See some of our top tips below to ensure you have the best chance of finding what you truly need.

- *Think of yourself as a 'catch'* – Beliefs directly influence thoughts, feelings and behaviour. Believing 'I'll never find true love' will make you think and act in ways that will block you from finding what you want; for example, 'I believe that I'm not attractive', 'I think that my partner is always looking over my shoulder for someone better-looking', or 'I act defensively and push people away'. Challenge these thinking patterns and replace negative thoughts with positive ones. Instead, say, 'I think that the conversation is going well', 'I'm attractive and unique' and 'I'm open to love'.

- *Like attracts like* – If you want to attract a loving, caring relationship into your life, you need to be positive and hopeful. When your actions are motivated by feelings of emptiness or lack of fulfilment, you will attract people with the same outlook and self-destructive actions. Instead, show yourself and the world the best you. Say to yourself that you are capable of a great life. Shout it from the rooftops!

- *Looking good* – This doesn't mean you have to be a size eight with blonde highlights; it means feeling good and looking the way you want the world to see you. If you prefer not to follow fashion, embrace that.

- *Heavy baggage* – Try not to let past mistakes and emotions into the present. If you need to work on issues from your past, see a professional therapist or counsellor.

- *Be confident* – When you meet someone you want to impress, put your best foot forward. Be proud of your accomplishments. Embrace the things about you that make you unique. If you don't feel that you're anything special, the other person won't either.

- *Give and take* – If you're going to be in a healthy, balanced relationship, as well as thinking about what you want, think about what you have to offer.

59. Eliminating insecurity

What one single personality trait makes you most popular, attractive and sexy? It's nothing to do with being tall, slim, beautiful, wealthy or ultra-intelligent; rather, it's everything to do with being *confident*. People are attracted to those with high self-esteem. If a woman or man genuinely believes in themselves (which should not be confused with arrogance), people are drawn to them instinctively.

Unfortunately, far too many people, rather than feeling confident, feel insecure. Insecurity stems from a wide variety of reasons. It can be as a result of overexposure to the culture of comparison so evident in today's consumerist society. It can be the result of an incidental hurtful comment made years earlier, such as being called fat or ugly or stupid. Sometimes people are driven to succeed to mask their insecurities – but no matter how successful you become, you will always want more from yourself as the insecurity driving you still remains.

The good news is that insecurities do not have to remain with you. To start with, you need to manage the source of your insecurity.

- Learn to think and speak differently. Don't pepper your talk with put-downs; find another way to converse. Remember, it's not your job to automatically fill any gaps in a conversation or provide amusement. When you fall into self-critical thoughts, note them. Once you are aware of them, make a deliberate effort to change them to positive thoughts; for example, by thinking about something you like about yourself.
- Avoid people who sap your self-esteem, either by putting you down or by building themselves up so much that you feel inferior. Instead, mix with people

who, because they believe in themselves, are secure enough to let you do the same.

- You may feel that you need to hide your successes – that you feel undeserving and unworthy. But it's vital to acknowledge them to yourself – and to let others realise you're doing well. So be proud of your victories, and share them with others. Celebrate and reinforce the message that you're worth it.

Know and develop yourself

- Try not to judge yourself by the things you can't control or lack; instead, focus on what's going on internally. Try to reset your expectations. Set yourself new challenges. For example, if you feel shy, join a reading group or some other type of activity that will let you ease into more social interaction. You can't develop if you never push your limits.

Look and act confident

- It's an old adage but feeling good about yourself on the inside will make you feel great on the outside. Small changes can give you that extra boost to your self-esteem.
- Use positive body language to appear more confident. Stand tall, be happy and approachable, be confident to take up space in your environment, keep an open and approachable posture and work to identify habits you display when you are nervous, like fidgeting. Most of us have one or two

unconscious 'tells' that give us away, but once we are aware of them we can consciously fix them.

- Ask for support – having family and friends to share our struggles and successes with makes our journey much easier and less intimidating. Accepting help from those who care about us will also strengthen our resilience and ability to manage stress.
- Anticipate obstacles – we will inevitably face them. However, anticipating obstacles ahead of time can help us stay on track.
- Don't beat yourself up – perfection is unattainable. Remember that minor missteps when reaching our goals are completely normal. We should resolve to recover from our mistakes and get back on track.

Attractiveness is about more than just having a pretty face, yet we usually think our physical appearance is most important when deciding whether or not we are attractive. Women tend to keep a close eye on their weight and they spend on average £36,000 on hair care over their lifetime. Men think about their stature, physique and hairline. We all have a tendency to focus on our appearance without realising that the pivotal factor in attractiveness is something entirely different: self-confidence.

When someone is confident within themselves, they transform the energy in the room. We are drawn to them; we want to be their friend, to talk to them – and to date them. In the world of dating, confidence is essential. Someone who doubts their own appearance and ability sends signals of insecurity that warn off potential partners. If you are dreary and dull, people will want to avoid you. If you are bright and vibrant, people will want to be around you.

There is, however, a thin line between confidence and arrogance. Overconfidence is a negative trait and a turn-off for most people. The quietly confident, self-assured person who is not afraid to show their vulnerability usually wins over the brash self-assurance of the overconfident.

60. How can you become more positive?

1) *Find a way to motivate yourself.* What helps you to feel happier in the morning? Find a way to incorporate this into your morning routine to start your day on a high.
2) *See the funny side of life.* When in a stressful situation try to take a moment and stop and reflect. What is the funny side of this situation?
3) *Manage stress better.* Exercise is one of the best forms of combating stress and raising your happiness levels. If the gym isn't your scene, why not try something different such as laughter yoga? You may want to incorporate breathing, visualisation or meditation into your workday to help you to relax.
4) *Make a 'positive' list.* Write a list of all the things in your life that are positive and make sure that you can see the list where you tend to be more stressed, such as work. Looking at this list should help you to feel happier and more relaxed.

5) *Treat yourself.* Make regular time for yourself where you can relax and enjoy yourself, whether it is a spot of retail therapy, meeting up with friends or a picnic in the park for one. Block this time out in your diary, if you have to. This will help you to realise that you are important too. It will also raise your self-esteem and make you feel happier.

6) *Explore your life.* Taking some time to explore your feelings is a great way to centre yourself when you feel stressed or down. For example, reflect on what is making you stressed: is it in certain situations or around certain people? Writing a diary where you note down events and your feelings in relation to them may be a good first step to trying to identify if there are any changes that you could make in your life that would make you happier.

7) *'Fake it until you make it!'* Research has shown that smiling can have a positive effect on your body and mood, whether it is a real or fake smile, since your brain doesn't know the difference. Therefore, by making a conscious effort to smile more, not only will you be more approachable, you will have the added benefit of feeling good. Just as fake smiling may make you start to feel happier, fake laughing also has the same effect on your state of mind as real laughter. Not only that, but over the long term this has other benefits, such as better health.

8) *Surround yourself with happy people.* If you surround yourself with happier and more positive people then

this is likely to affect your mindset, and make you happier as well.

9) *Focus on your own life.* Stay focused on your own goals and on what you want from life rather than comparing yourself to others. There will always be someone who is financially or socially more successful than you are. Next time you start to compare yourself, try thinking of it this way – every minute you spend thinking about someone else is less time that you have spent on your own life and success.

10) *Increase your positive thoughts.* Notice when you are having negative thoughts and try to think of two positive thoughts to counteract this. Retrain your brain and thought patterns so they work for you rather than against you. After all, it is your mind!

11) *Make time to play!* Yes, even adults can benefit from making time to play, whether this is with friends, children or partner. Incorporating more playfulness into your life increases the chance of laughter with the people who are special to you, which can improve your relationships with them.

12) *Increase physical touch in your intimate relationships.* Various psychological research studies have shown that physical contact, such as hugging and kissing, has physiological benefits and can improve psychological wellbeing.

61. The psychology of stress and relaxation

Some people are naturally more relaxed than others. However, what one person may find relaxing may be very different to what another person finds relaxing.

Relaxation is a state of being that we all desire and require from time to time. To be relaxed means to be in an emotional state that presents itself with the absence of any tension.

In the 1960s, much psychological research showed the positive effects that relaxation has on health and mental health; specifically, it was found to have a positive impact on anxiety and many other areas relating to such things as sleep disorders, depression and eating disorders.

A relaxing activity provides relief from tension. For example, some people benefit by exercising, which releases adrenalin and serotonin into the body. Others benefit from social interaction, meditation, taking a walk somewhere scenic, or talking with a therapist of life coach.

However, some people find it hard to relax. This may be because they engage in destructive behaviour, such as drug or alcohol abuse, or because they find it both mentally and physically impossible to release control to the point that they can relax.

If this sounds like you, get in touch with an experienced psychologist or life coach, who will able to show you the best methods and tools to feel relaxed for longer and more often.

62. How to beat the office blues

Stress within the workplace is an ongoing problem experienced by many professionals, and it can be hard to not let it influence your personal life. A major source of stress is a lack of free time to spend with family and friends. This has a negative impact on both physical and mental wellbeing.

Seventy Thirty has come up with a few tips to beat the office blues and potentially repair those close relationships we may be unknowingly harming.

- *Always look on the bright side of life*! For two weeks, take five minutes each day to think of seven things you are grateful for in life; these may be anything from enjoying good health to having a relaxing journey to work.

- *Unwind with some music* – make a playlist of your favourite, upbeat songs. When you are feeling stressed, pop on your headphones and let yourself become immersed in the music. The experience of positive emotions when listening to music acts as a buffer against the effects of negative emotions, thus reducing stress levels.

- *Show them some love* – if you know you will be stuck at work for most of the day and the evening, call a loved one during your lunch break to share a positive story with them. Tell them that you love them, or plan a fun activity for later in the week. It will remind them that, although you may not be physically present, you are very much emotionally present.

- *Reclaim Mondays* – many of us find Monday mornings the most challenging time of the week, so when you have a spare five minutes, take the time to think about something you are looking forward to. If there is nothing positive at all, this should be the motivation you need to start looking for a job you enjoy! Most of our life is spent working, so it's important that you love your work and are passionate about it.

- *Express yourself* – expressing our emotions, instead of repressing them, has been found to increase and prolong positive emotions and act as a cushion against negative emotions. So when you do any of the above tasks, make sure you express the emotions you are feeling at the time. Hiding emotions, positive or negative, does no one any good.

PART EIGHT: How to resolve relationship problems

63. The psychology of jealousy

'Plain women are always jealous of their husbands. Beautiful women never are. They are always so occupied with being jealous of other women's husbands.' – Oscar Wilde

Evolutionary psychology has shown us that men and women value different characteristics in a partner. Men value physical attractiveness in women because a woman's physical attractiveness is related to her fertility, whereas women value dominance in men as it is related to a man's ability to provide resources.

Like many emotional adaptations, jealousy is a flawed and often exaggerated call to arms. That is because the human life span was, until not long ago, much shorter than it is now. Evolutionary psychologists and anthropologists believe that our ancestors rarely got a second chance to woo a mate. Our ancestors succeeded in acquiring mates long enough to procreate – those who couldn't are ancestors to no one. It makes sense then that humans developed jealousy as a built-in infidelity-detection system, in this competitive social cauldron.

What causes jealousy?

- A person with low self-esteem may view themselves as less competitive among a same-sex group than they really are. In extreme situations they may feel so undeserving of being loved that they can't believe that their spouse could possibly remain faithful to them.
- Feelings of insecurity may stem from low self-esteem, or may be related to instances in which we have previously been hurt.
- A fear of vulnerability is the inability to let our guard down and let another person know us completely.
- Distrust.
- Uncertainty and loneliness.

How do you stop jealousy?

1. Make an effort to no longer engage in self-defeating behaviour. If you are questioning or making accusations, stop the behaviour immediately. Whether you need to literally bite your tongue, go to another room, or talk to a friend, don't allow yourself to continue with this destructive behaviour. Usually people engage in self-defeating behaviour because initially it is reassuring to them and makes them feel better. But remind yourself that feeling better is just temporary and that it is a destructive behaviour that must stop.

2. Challenge your irrational thinking styles frequently. Identify how your thinking is irrational, and remind yourself whenever you have these jealous thoughts. It is often beneficial to write this down. On closer inspection, it may be

more obvious to you there is no reason to be jealousy, or that there is evidence to the contrary, such as the loving things your spouse does for you.

3. Work on improving your self-esteem. Remember that jealousy is not about others, but about you. Use the presence of jealous feelings to remind yourself that you need to focus on improving your self-esteem. Give yourself positive self-statements and engage in behaviours that make you feel good about yourself.

4. Learn to be vulnerable and to develop emotional intimacy. For any relationship to be successful, you must be able to take risks. There are many ways to do this. For instance, if you feel insecure, you might share these feelings with your partner and talk about ways they can help you feel more secure. Or, if you are afraid of being vulnerable, try to share this worry with your partner.

Sometimes the process of developing awareness and challenging irrational beliefs can be too difficult to accomplish alone, and you may need assistance from a therapist. A good cognitive behavioural therapist will be able to help you with these types of worries and doubts. They can help you identify where you are going wrong. Are you engaging in so much negative self-talk that you need help to change this destructive behaviour? Do you have unresolved issues from a previous relationship? Do you lack self-confidence and have a low perception of yourself? Jealousy can destroy a relationship and can stem from a wide combination of all of the above. However, with help, you can get back on the road of positivity and make current or future relationships work. By using techniques designed to help address the issue from a wide range of perspectives, you will also be better able to establish what went wrong. This will give you the self-awareness to halt any destructive behaviour in the future.

64. 'You could do so much better'

Our nearest and dearest often think they know what's best for us. But finding a partner is hard enough, so what do you do when you meet someone new and your loved ones do not approve of your new partner?

With parental figures especially, you may find that they will take an instant dislike to anyone you bring home, simply because no one is 'good enough' for you. Friends may disapprove because they don't want to lose their 'partner in crime'.

In many cases, family and friends just need to have more time to get to know your partner, so it becomes clear why you love each other. In other cases, due to social or cultural reasons, perhaps, nothing you do will make a difference to how your family and friends feel. Take time to reflect on the situation and make sure you feel confident in your choice (whether to stay with your partner or to leave them) and why. It is important to take into account your needs and desires, but also the role of family and friends and your place in the community.

However, you may be in an unhealthy relationship and, because love is blind, fail to notice it or choose to ignore it. Destructive relationships can result in a myriad of negative consequences: you may lose friends, find you have less interest in things you used to enjoy, or take on negative coping strategies (such as drinking). This won't go unnoticed by your loved ones and, because they care about you, they will let you know about it.

When in a relationship, you are likely to show some behavioural changes. These can be positive changes, such as being more active or sociable. Whether the change is good or bad, it usually causes some anxiety for your loved ones. You have to work out whether their anxiety stems from wanting to preserve their relationship with you, or whether it is because they feel the need to protect you.

Relationships can be tricky at the best of times, and they are all the more difficult when your loved ones disapprove of your partner. Here are some tips from Seventy Thirty to help in this situation.

-   It is important to remember that, more often than not, those closest to you will be looking out for your best interests. If your loved ones provide solid reasons why they do not think your partner is right for you (e.g. they may be controlling or possessive) then it may be worthwhile taking a step back from the situation to see if there is any truth in what they are telling you.

- Introduce your partner to your loved ones gradually. If you have brought home a few different potential partners, your loved ones may not think to take your relationship seriously. Or they may assume the worst and 'paint them with the same brush' as previous partners who may not have been right for you. Bring up your partner in conversation with your family and friends. After a while, they will realise that this person is an important part of your life and be more accepting when they meet them.

- If your loved ones are openly rude about your partner, sit down with them one to one and ask them why they dislike your partner. Try to reassure them that their assumptions are wrong, that this person makes you very happy. The reason behind loved ones interfering may be because they are afraid of losing you and scared of your relationship changing. Make sure to keep in contact with them and set aside some one-on-one time to make them feel valued. However, it is very important that you make this on your own terms; do not let them take advantage of your kindness and sacrifice the time that you should be investing in your relationship.

- We often vent to those closest to us whenever our partner does something wrong, but fail to tell them about all the good things he does. If you are always passing on negative information about your partner, those closest to you will form a very one-sided view of him. Stop focusing on the negative and start telling people about all the nice things your partner does for you too.

- If all else fails, remember ignorance can be bliss. When a member of your family or close friend makes a derogatory comment about your partner, ignore it and change the subject; make sure that your partner does the same. Soon your loved ones will come to realise that your partner is a part of your life and nothing will change that. Once they have realised this, their behaviour should subside.

All close relationships are valuable and need to be nurtured. If you and your partner break up, you will need your friends and family to help you pick up the pieces. Not all relationships will work out, no matter how much we try. However, if you're in a healthy relationship and your loved ones know how important your partner is to you, they will learn to accept them. They may even grow to like them.

65. The self-disconnector

The self-disconnector – someone who has had negative emotional experiences that have made her feel unlovable. They feel unworthy. They believe what their ex-partner(s) say about their flaws.

Result: they detaches from their 'worth' and try to find it in their partners instead.

What sort of life experiences can make us behave this way?

We normally develop habitual patterns very early in our lives. Psychologists believe that these relationship patterns are developed between birth and seven years old – the imprint period. They are learned unconsciously as a result of the relationships we have with our primary caregivers. It is thought that whatever we learn at the unconscious level at this age will stay with us and affect our behaviour and choices throughout our lives (unless we become aware of these patterns and act to address any negative ones).

Being rejected by someone who features heavily in your life as a child or having an absent parent can be the most important reasons for an individual feeling that they are not worth people's time and attention, or that they are unlovable.

Some individuals will be more self-aware and may be able to reflect and unlearn this kind of thought pattern. But if someone believes they are unlovable it will always play out in their relationships. Usually this can be seen in the type of people they are unconsciously attracted to – someone they believe is too good for them whom they place on a pedestal. They don't often set healthy boundaries, and tend to become co-dependent, believing that without their partner they are worth nothing. This type of mindset also means that they are more likely to absorb and believe any criticism and negative feedback.

What are the best ways to stop this behaviour?

The more we know about ourselves, the more choices we have. We can then *choose* not to behave in a certain way. We have to be willing to see the part we play in attracting certain relationship issues into our lives. If you struggle with this, ask a couple of your closest friends to write down a paragraph describing you. Others tend to see negative behaviour patterns more easily than we do in ourselves.

The core of this is the tendency to base your relationships on what you think you deserve, as opposed to what you really deserve, and what is healthy. One good way to think about your next choice of partner is to focus on finding people who share your values, beliefs and goals.

If you are in a relationship that is not working for any of the above reasons, and you still think there is hope that it can be positive – reset the boundaries. It's likely that you have given your partner far too much leeway and always put yourself second. It can come as a shock to a partner who has had an easy time in the relationship in terms of getting things their way, but you will need to be firm. If the relationship is worth saving, they will want you to feel more confident and secure.

The fixator – this is the type of person who has never wanted to support themselves or be independent on a financial or emotional level. As mentioned before, this might not be an issue for everyone, but if you want to grow as a person the time will come when you need to address this and develop your own personality and character. However, change can be difficult, as people with this type of characteristic often stay in relationships that are not fulfilling because they fear change.

If a person is secure in this type of relationship and feels comfortable and happy with it, there is no reason why it should not work. The problem here is that these women, or men, may have chosen their partners to make up for shortcomings in their own lives (such as an inability to be independent and look after themselves) rather than partners who are right for them in terms of their personal development (someone who would encourage this).

Practical tip – how do you break this pattern and find love in a healthy way?

Address the underdeveloped parts of your self – try to realise that it is not someone else's job to complete you. A shift of focus from the couple to the self is a good first step towards greater independence.

The shadow victim – this person attracts partners who reflect the parts that they reject in themselves. The *shadow* is a psychological term coined by the late Swiss psychiatrist, Dr Carl Jung. It is everything in us that is unconscious, repressed, undeveloped and denied. Jung believed that we desire to be whole (reunited with our unconscious elements) but that, instead of facing up to these things in ourselves, we unconsciously attract these things in the partner we choose. This results in 'projection' – a psychological defence mechanism whereby one projects their undesirable thoughts, motivations, desires and feelings onto someone else.

Consider a person, who is part of a couple, who is thinking about infidelity. Instead of dealing with these undesirable thoughts consciously, they subconsciously project these feelings onto the other person and begin to think that the *other* has thoughts of infidelity and may be having an affair. In this way, one can see that projection is related to denial, arguably the only defence mechanism that is more primitive than projection. Those who project their feelings deny a part of themselves. In this case, they cannot face their own feelings of infidelity and therefore project them onto the other person.

How can you tell if you are experiencing a 'shadow relationship'?

We have all had many painful, difficult experiences which have clearly looked like it is the other person's fault, or bad luck in life, or whatever else we want to call it. If you are experiencing this type of relationship time and time again, it is unlikely that you are taking full responsibility for the choices you make.

Practical tip – how can you break the pattern?

The first thing is to take responsibility for your life. Depending on how self-aware you are, this can be straightforward or it can be difficult. Of course, people who have very little self-awareness may not recognise this kind of behaviour in themselves.

Look out for situations arising between yourself and other people to whom you are very different. Notice how often this happens. If it happens regularly, then you may need to reflect on and modify your behaviour. Working your way through this to a healthy relationship requires both partners moving towards the middle of the polarisation. It requires a commitment from both sides and a desire to have a positive relationship.

66. Does the rescuer need rescuing?

There are some people, known as *rescuers*, who repeatedly find themselves in relationships with partners who are needy, emotionally damaged or going through a particularly difficult point in their life. These personal challenges are usually at odds with the rescuer's relationship goals, values and beliefs, yet instead of recognising this incompatibility and moving on, the rescuer attempts to fix, or save, their partner. This is undertaken based on the usually misguided belief or hope that, with their help, their partner can be fixed and become the person they really want them to be. Seldom does this happen. In reality, giving your all to fix, change or save your partner, especially when your effort and energy is not reciprocated, will ultimately leave you drained, resentful and unfulfilled. Eventually you will feel like you have no other option but to leave. You may then promise yourself that you will not try to fix another person from within a relationship again. You may resolve to find a partner who will support you too, rather than it always being the other way round. However, sure enough, you find yourself in a relationship with someone who may have a different set of circumstances but ultimately the same issue arises; you find yourself trying to save them.

Why do we choose partners we feel we have to save?

Why do so many of us make the same mistakes again and again when it comes to people we date? We see our friends in loving relationships with partners who look after and support them but can never seem to find this for ourselves.

Repeated psychological studies have found that the relationships we have with our caregivers and significant people in our lives at key stages of development (infancy, childhood and adolescence) have a great impact on the selections we make with regard to our adult romantic relationships. One of the main streams of research in agreement with this focuses on attachment theory.

Although attachment history may be one of the underlying causes of people repeating the same relationship patterns, these choices are not inevitable; patterns can be consciously broken. For example, one potential reason for someone repeatedly selecting partners who need saving is that they may have developed an early attachment to a particularly dominant, controlling figure. If they felt this was a negative experience, they may go to great pains as an adult to avoid relationships with partners they feel could put them in the same position, thus being drawn to relationships in which they feel needed and in the position of control. Consequently, they will tend to choose weaker partners who they perceive as needing to be looked after. However, on an unconscious level their attachment history is driving them towards a relationship with a stronger character who will be more dominating and powerful (as with their infant relationship). This incongruence in conscious and unconscious needs and drivers means that rescuers will eventually get tired of playing the supportive half of the partnership as their hearts are not fully in it.

How can we change these patterns of behaviour?

The best way to break this pattern of behaviour is to sit down and look at all the significant relationships in your life. Spend some time reflecting on what they taught you, what you want and what you need from a future relationship. In doing so, you are taking the first steps in integrating your conscious and unconscious drivers and can start to think more clearly about the type of relationship that will work best for you.

Successful relationships are built upon shared value systems, relationship goals, backgrounds and physical attraction, among many other factors. Therefore, try focusing on these things to help you make the right decisions.

67. Time to talk

We've all had silly arguments with our partners. Precious minutes, hours and even days can be wasted feeling upset and angry over a fight or overthinking the things you said: 'I wish I'd said that differently!' 'Why did I say that?' 'I didn't really mean it!'

What can we do in order to avoid arguments like this?

- *Are you hungry/sleep deprived?* It's normal to be irritable and distracted if our basic needs are not fulfilled, such as lack of food or sleep. Be sure to consider whether your feelings are being exacerbated by your biological needs. Walk away from the problem for now and come back to it when you are feeling more yourself.
- *Is it the right time?* Sometimes we don't really think things through; we jump to conclusions and get into an argument on the defence. We may later realise that it actually wasn't that important or that we could have handled it differently. It's sometimes best to cool off and reflect on what caused the initial distress; give your partner time to do the same too. Being a couple also means respecting each other's vital space and meeting each other halfway.
- *Don't make it personal.* The most long-lasting damage that arises from arguments is when a fight becomes personal. Try to stick to the problem in the most objective way possible. Demoralising or insulting your partner with contempt or sarcasm, or

making fun of their looks, intelligence, job, or family is not behaviour worthy of a loving relationship. Keep away from generalising comments such as 'You always...' or 'You never...' which project a negative light onto your partner's personality rather than the specific matter at hand. This will only result in a defensive reaction and consequent mutual criticism. All you will achieve is a negative competitive spiral that will take you and your partner into a worse situation that than it was originally.

- *Communicate.* Letting the other person explain themselves, maintaining eye contact, being understanding and showing mutual respect (not interrupting or walking out of the room) have been proven to be effective ways of disentangling a problem and fully understanding each other.

Remember that you are not there to judge what your partner is saying is true or false. All their feelings are valid, even if you do not agree with them. For example, if your partner feels that you been neglecting him/her, listen to why they feel this way. In turn try and explain how you feel. Keep the conversation open and communicative. Don't walk away or sulk. Try to be objective and don't resent your partner for communicating their feelings to you.

All couples argue sometimes. In fact, arguments dealt with in a healthy adult way can lead to a stronger relationship. When all you want to do is stamp your feet and shout, remember that having a healthy communication style will help you and your partner to solve any problems more quickly and will lead to a more satisfactory relationship for you both.

68. Emotional blackmail in a relationship

Many children discover that crying, even if it is not genuine or heartfelt, will elicit the response they are looking for, such as getting to stay up later, or the toy they want in a shop. This is relatively normal and, as they grow, most children learn that there are better ways of asking for things they want. Some adults, however, still practise this type of toxic emotional blackmail. It comes in many forms, from using emotion to control others through accessing their feelings of guilt, to threatening a loved one with withdrawal of your love if they do not give you what you want. Emotional blackmail is a powerful form of manipulation. Typically, emotional blackmailers will know us very well indeed and will be aware of all our weaknesses and areas of vulnerability. They may have a demand they know we are unlikely to comply with and may use threats, or play on past circumstances they know are likely to cause guilt. A typical example of this type of emotional bullying is to say, 'You obviously don't love me as much as I love you', or, 'If we can't agree on this, perhaps we should call it quits.'

The usual response to emotional blackmail is to try and resist, followed by some form of compliance – because of how much we value the relationship and because the blackmailer has usually pressed all the right buttons, with a detailed knowledge of our weak spots. Unfortunately, once someone has succeeded in using this technique in a relationship, a pattern can develop. Indeed, typically emotional blackmail is characterised by repetition and continuity. When you surrender to a blackmailer's emotional threats, an unpleasant cycle will develop in a relationship, which becomes progressively difficult to stop. As a victim you can lose all sense of boundaries and end up agreeing to things that you do not want to agree with.

This can slowly destroy a person, as they lose their sense of self and become immersed in a relationship where they have little control, thus become even more vulnerable. Partners who use emotional blackmail are generally narcissistic, with little ability for self-reflection or an understanding of personal responsibility. If you find your partner uses emotional blackmail as a normal part of your relationship, it is wise to bring this to their attention and seek couples counselling. If they do not agree to work on this issue or continue to use emotional bullying tactics, it is best to leave them and seek support from family and friends or professionals. In order to preserve your sense of self-worth, it is important to realise that someone who is narcissistic is unlikely to ever change, or provide what you need to ensure a healthy loving relationship.

69. The unemotional partner

Everybody feels emotions; however, how well people express their emotions varies from person to person. *Emotional availability* means when a person is able to share their feelings with another person. An unemotional person is out of touch with their emotions and is unable to define or express them in a healthy way.

Why are people sometimes unemotional?

Often the ways that we express emotions are learned in childhood. The unemotional person may not have been taught how to express their emotions as a child, or emotional expression may have been discouraged. In addition, for men, the expression of emotions may be perceived to be unmanly. For example, a boy may be taught that 'big boys don't cry', so they may see showing emotions as a sign of weakness. In addition, they may feel scared and insecure about expressing their emotions as perhaps they have been hurt in the past. The unemotional person may have a fear of losing control if they express their emotions. Emotions can be unpredictable and an unemotional person may feel safer intellectualising their experiences through the use of logic rather than allowing themselves to feel. In this way, they may find it more comfortable to internalise or rationalise their emotions to themselves rather than to express them.

How does emotional unavailability affect a relationship?

Often, it is the emotionally available partner who is more impacted by this dynamic and they can be affected in the following ways.

- They may feel insecure in the relationship and unsupported by their unemotional partner.
- They may feel rejected or unloved when their partner avoids speaking about their feelings, or walks away from conflict.
- There may be a breakdown in communication, as the emotionally available person may feel as if they are not 'allowed' to express their emotions either. This can lead to the development of many unresolved issues within the relationship.
- Emotional connection is an important aspect of a relationship. When this is not there, the emotionally available person may feel distant, detached or cut off from their partner, and also unheard, as their partner may be unresponsive when it comes to talking about emotions.
- Continual feelings of rejection can impact upon the self-esteem of the emotionally available person, which can lead to feelings of not being good enough, isolation and loneliness.
- A lack of emotional expression may also mean that there is a lack of intimacy in the relationship. For example, the unemotional partner may not initiate physical gestures of affection such as hugs or kisses. Instead, they may express their feelings in other

ways, such as buying their partner presents instead of saying 'I love you'.

- There may be a lack of empathy in the relationship as the unemotional person struggles to understand the feelings of their partner. This can lead to the emotional person feeling misunderstood.
- The unemotional person may express their emotions in an unhealthy way. For example, they may bottle up unexpressed feelings until they erupt in anger, or avoid talking about their feelings by burying their heads in the sand. They may hope that in this way any conflicts or issues will disappear, However, this often only makes things worse.
- The unemotional person may also have developed unhealthy ways of dealing with their emotions, such as using drugs or alcohol to help them to block out their feelings, which will further negatively impact upon their relationship.

How to cope with the unemotional person: what can be done?

- Healthy relationships consist of balance, as one person cannot meet all of our needs. It is important to keep a range of interests outside the relationship. This can provide an important social network for the emotionally available partner and it also removes unhealthy pressure from the relationship.

- Find an activity that you enjoy doing together and bring the fun back into your relationship, as this is a first step towards building intimacy. Spending regular quality time together can help strengthen your emotional connection. Communication is another important aspect of a relationship, and open communication will help to build trust.
- Communication does not always have to be verbal. Non-verbal communication, such as body language and eye contact, is a powerful way of encouraging an unemotional person to express their emotions. They may find it easier to show their emotions rather than talk about them. Learning more about your partner's non-verbal communication can help you to understand more clearly what they are trying to say to you.
- Break patterns of behaviour and try something new. If you can identify the problems within a relationship, it will give you the power to make good choices and to break repeat patterns of negative behaviour. As a couple, you can begin to identify each other's needs within the relationship. It is not just about learning about yourself, but also learning about your partner and how to support them. Look at what is missing or lacking from your relationship, whether this is passion, commitment or intimacy, and discuss practical ways to make positive changes.
- Another important tool is modelling your emotions. In other words, if you want your partner to express their emotions in a healthy way, then you need to

express yourself in this way first. One way could be to use 'I' statements when expressing your emotions, such as, 'I feel that...'. By expressing your emotions in this way, your partner is less likely to feel attacked, is more likely to understand your point of view and may be more open to talking about their emotions in the same way.

- Focus on your present emotions and feelings – avoid bringing up past conflicts or arguments. By focusing on the here and now, you are more likely to understand each other and move towards finding a solution.

- Take the time to listen. When we have strong emotions, we may feel hurt and want our point of view to be heard. This can mean we become defensive and may not hear our partner's point of view. In this case, both people in a relationship may feel misunderstood. Try and listen to what your partner is saying without interrupting them, rather than becoming defensive. You are more likely to understand your partner in this way, and they are more likely to understand you. Remember, it takes two people to make a relationship work.

- At times it may be easier to work on emotional expression in a neutral environment. You may want to seek professional help and to see a couples therapist together if you are both willing to work on your relationship. Individual therapy may also be beneficial in providing you a space to heal from emotional issues.

70. Anger analysis

Some anger is healthy. Anger has an evolutionary value: it allows us to fight back when necessary and to stand up for ourselves in life. We have probably all found ourselves in situations where we feel angry and have found that this anger is actually doing us much more harm than good. There are times we don't want to be angry, or it doesn't serve us to be angry; when we can get a better result by being considerate and calm. It is only possible to achieve this by taking responsibility for our own anger.

Once you are aware that your anger is your responsibility, the key is to catch initial anger-inducing thoughts and replace them with a conscious interpretation of the information. For example, if your partner plans to go out with their friends rather than staying in and having dinner at home with you, rather than immediately assuming the worst ('She *knew* I wanted a quiet night in!', or 'I *knew* he didn't want to spend any quality time with me!'), take a more considered stance. Until you are able to discuss it together, give your partner the benefit of the doubt. Think of alternative reasons why your partner may have chosen to go out, such as 'Perhaps he didn't realise I was hoping to have a quiet night in tonight', or 'She did say she was hoping to see her friends this week'. Remember, long-term healthy relationships are based on trust and respect.

By becoming aware of which thoughts trigger your anger, you can actively choose to balance your thinking and control your own emotions. It really is this simple.

71. Venting your frustrations in a relationship

By definition, *venting* is a term used to allude to an outlet or exit from confinement. It is also a concept used to describe the expression of intense emotion, often with the purpose of liberating oneself of pent-up frustration.[12]

When it comes to relationships, we are often confronted with certain inconsistencies that threaten imbalance as our reality fails to match our expectations, leaving us agitated and obstructing the flow of positive energy exchange with our partner. *Frustration* is a negative emotion related to dissatisfaction, anger or disappointment. In this respect, the purpose of venting frustration is emancipation. Theoretically, this should lead to freedom from angst. However, this is not always the case.

Before understanding how to effectively deal with venting your frustrations in a relationship, we must psychologically assess *why* we feel the way we do. This allows us to create a stronger foundation when building a successful, fulfilling relationship.

Self-awareness

The first step to your journey in uncovering truth involves self-awareness. Often frustration is a side-effect of deeper issues we are experiencing within ourselves. In an attempt to resolve this, we may find that we subconsciously project our feelings on to our partner. We may feel insecure,

---

[12] http://www.thefreedictionary.com/venting.

jealous, paranoid or anxious, but whichever undesirable emotion is preoccupying our thoughts and influencing our behaviours, we must learn to first recognise it and then separate it from our relationship with our partner, unless of course it is inextricably interlinked to their direct actions.

Seek guidance

It may be helpful to seek guidance from a non-biased, trusted friend or family member in whom you can confide. This will enable you to determine whether your level of frustration is rational or slightly delusional, as this unhealthy emotion can taint your clarity and perception. In this way, you have discussed the situation at least once before you decide to confront your partner, already helping you to focus your thoughts more logically and, hopefully, harnessing your emotions so that you do not aggressively handle the internal conflict you are experiencing. If you feel the need to cry, get angry or act in any other way to feel better, do it. You may also find it therapeutic to exercise, pamper yourself or write down your thoughts.

Release versus expression

There is a clear balance between release and expression, and how you vent your frustration is related directly to how you will feel post-vent. Understanding yourself, controlling your outbursts and speaking only once you have concrete evidence that justifies your frustration will help the outcome of your interaction to be positive. *Release* implies setting free, allowing to escape. *Expression* denotes a more articulate manifestation of ideas, a mindful conveying of sensibilities, a selfless process by which we think first and act upon our pre-contemplations without the urge to give in to an impulse for instant gratification. By choosing expression over release, we can move forward positively with our partner, feeing re-energised and liberated in the relationship.

By choosing the former, we are proactively making the decision to grow stronger through our pain rather than suffer as a result of it.

Venting as an opportunity

Using venting as an opportunity is critical, not only in understanding *yourself* better but also in understanding your *self-worth*, because you *deserve* the very best. Although frustration is unhealthy, having and feeling emotion is not. It's what makes us human. Perhaps there is a highly valid cause for this preoccupation and you should address it frankly if an issue is persistently on your mind. In a relationship, we hear the overused concept of how important *communication* is; however, its strength is very rarely put into practice. Discussing your feelings openly and honestly with your partner can relieve stress in ways beyond your immediate comprehension. We all need emotional validation from time to time, so be mindful that what you are feeling is completely fine and is a basic human need that *needs* to be fulfilled in order for you to feel happy and secure.[13]

Ultimately, *venting frustration in a relationship* should be done with integrity and respect. Act according to your

[13] http://www.psychologytoday.com/blog/the-squeaky-wheel/201106/the-antidote-anger-and-frustration.

values, try to understand the situation from the other person's perspective, and remember that your approach should always be expressed with the goal of a positive outcome. Releasing emotions in anger threatens your relationship and once you have acted, you cannot take your outburst back, so ensure you are true to yourself and fair to your partner.

72. Dating after cancer – the role of optimism and honesty

Being diagnosed with cancer is a devastating experience. As well as having to deal with the physical aspects of the experience, the psychological impact can be multi-faceted. It strikes at the heart of our self, our body image and, correspondingly, at our levels of self-esteem and confidence. However, adopting a positive and open approach can help to improve and protect your psychological and physical wellbeing, both important factors when considering moving on with your life and exploring new relationships.

Optimism and gratitude

Feelings of anxiety naturally occur when we are faced with a negative life event, such as being diagnosed with cancer, and it is normal to feel as though it has had a debilitating effect on moving forward with life goals. Anxiety can result in a cycle of negative thinking that may involve worry and a loss of self-esteem.

A first step towards getting back into dating after surviving cancer is to be aware that you are powerful. You have been though a life-changing situation and come out the other side and now you are stronger for it.

Some guidance

1. Before you start dating, acknowledge the positive aspects of your physical being. Provide yourself with the healthy nourishment it needs and the exercise that it deserves. Regularly exercising and eating a diet rich in fruit and vegetables and healthy fats will help you to look after your physical and your psychological wellbeing and will result in the production of natural mood-enhancing chemicals, including increased levels of serotonin and endorphins.

2. Be sincere and honest in your feelings towards dating. Practise open and honest communication and connection by discussing your fears about disclosure with a trusted friend. Practise getting those fears out into the open; it will become less difficult if you have aired them verbally in advance. Choose when your story should be revealed to a potential partner. Do not feel that you are withholding information; rather, instead you are taking the time to establish some trust between you both first.

3. Practise gratitude of any kind, including expressing your appreciation of the support that you have

received from friends, family and the professionals who have helped you survive this experience.

4. Develop an optimistic view on life. Challenge any negative thoughts and know that, even if you are not a naturally optimistic person, by continually replacing negative thoughts with their more positive alternative, you will strengthen your positivity.

Developing both a *cognitive style* and a *lifestyle* that facilitate positivity, and having a sincere and honest approach to dating, will increase your physical and mental wellbeing.

73. Dating techniques

'I have terrible dating techniques, and I am struggling to find a partner. Please give me some professional tips.' – Anna

Let's have a look at Seventy Thirty's list of dating techniques.

1   Have a clear picture of what you want in, and from, a relationship.

2   Know your type: make sure you matchmake yourself correctly.

3   Learn how to have meaningful conversations: know when to speak, and how to do it appropriately, while chatting to millionaires.

4   Don't rush into sex.

5   Don't talk about money.

6   Be mysterious: honesty and openness are not the same thing!
7   Be happy, cheerful and secure.
8   Be supportive and understanding.
9   Appreciate him: don't resent him or argue with him about his commitments.
10   Social etiquette: have the confidence to interact with and impress people at high-profile parties.
11   Have the right image: look, feel and act the part.

After writing to us, Anna had life coaching/date coaching sessions with one of our matchmakers. Anna is a 31-year-old executive in a large software company. She has worked very hard for her success and is very proud of her achievements. However, spending lots of time studying and working meant Anna had devoted less time to socialising and having fun. With respect to her values, background and relationship goals, we felt Anna would best suit a successful gentleman who would understand her drive and ambition. Anna stated that she was 'not having much luck finding the right partner' and she was wondering why. She felt that her dates were all good, fun and exciting, and she couldn't understand why the men she met didn't call her again.

The first thing we spotted, when we began our work with her, was that Anna talked and talked. She rarely asked any questions. It also became clear that she had not taken any time out to understand herself and the type of man she would be most suited to. When Anna described her dates, we paid careful attention. Anna was not following a number of the steps above. She didn't know her 'type', she wasn't well practised in the art of meaningful conversation, and she talked so much that she was most definitely not mysterious. Additionally, she spent so much time talking that she had no time to be supportive and encouraging towards her date.

After doing some work on values and relationship goals to enable Anna to reflect on what she wanted in a relationship, we engaged her in role play. She was asked to remember her last date (as though she was there, in the moment) and to describe everything she was seeing. Anna was able to do this with no problems; she described the man sitting opposite her, a beautiful restaurant full of people, the food and the wine. We then asked her to describe everything she was feeling. Anna described a feeling of 'nervous excitement' and also something that she described as 'anxiety'. She said that the anxiety related to a fear that the conversation wouldn't flow and an anticipation of awkward silences. When Anna was asked to describe everything she was hearing, as we had expected (by the amount she talked), she struggled. She could clearly hear herself talking, the chatter in the background and some soft music, but she never once referred to hearing her date's voice.

Anna was then asked to move to the other side of the table and to literally step into the shoes of her date. She was asked to see everything that he saw (she described herself on the other side of the table), and then we asked what he was hearing. This was the point at which she began to notice that she had been the one talking all the time – about herself. We then asked Anna to imagine how her date was feeling during the dinner. She was horrified when she thought about things from his perspective, and felt his frustration at not being able to get a word in. She commented that he wouldn't have known she was nervous as he didn't know her. She also said that he probably felt that Anna was 'selfish and inconsiderate'.

Anna then stepped into the shoes of one of the restaurant staff, enabling her to see the date from yet another perspective. When she described the situation from the perspective of an outsider looking at the couple, she mentioned that the man with her was a very successful chap. She said that he looked as though he was hard-working and he probably wanted to spend time with an attentive lady, to enjoy himself, to have fun and to 'blow off some steam'.

As we had already worked with Anna on her 'type', this exercise was the beginning of her journey to learn how she could improve her dating techniques. Anna later said, 'I can't believe I didn't see it before. It really is no surprise those guys run away from me. They like to be made to feel special, and I do my best to diminish my own anxiety and end up making myself feel special!'

Anna's communications skills are now much better, and she is dating successfully.

74. How to maintain a healthy relationship and give your existing relationship an MOT

Successful long-term relationships involve ongoing effort and compromise by both partners. Since relationship skills are rarely 'taught', sometimes one or both partners may not know how to establish, and maintain, a healthy and mutually satisfying relationship.

Dianna is a 35-year-old lawyer who has always aspired to the finer things in life and to finding a lovely, financially successful partner. She met Brian, a 43-year-old architect and business owner who is very wealthy and comes from a wealthy family. In contrast, Dianna has struggled financially at times during her life and has run up large debts. Brian was very generous and, from the start of their relationship, he spent lots of money on Dianna. Very soon, Dianna had changed her focus of attention to Brian's money, because she liked the way she felt every time Brian gave her an expensive present. Nine months into their relationship, Dianna was hooked on money, yet she had also become impatient and argumentative with Brian and she began to start refusing sex. She behaved like a spoilt child, demanding presents and expensive holidays. In the end, Brian broke up with her, despite liking her a lot before her new behaviour patterns kicked in. Warning: you can become hooked on money just as you can on drugs. Money brings both pleasure and power.

Rob and Sasha are a pleasant young couple who hope to marry. Sasha comes from a humble background and is not highly educated, whereas Rob comes from a well-off family, attended an expensive private school and is a university graduate. Their relationship is loving and caring, but Sasha was damaging the relationship because of her insecurities. Every time they went out and Rob entered into conversation with a more educated woman, Sasha would become jealous and start fighting with him. Sasha would attack Rob, insult him and fire off accusations. The relationship was at breaking point; Rob was not happy to continue having arguments about this and Sasha couldn't help herself.

We had to spend time with Sasha to find out exactly what her beliefs around this insecurity were, and challenge the beliefs that were not useful to her. Sasha believed that Rob found educated and sophisticated women attractive. When we asked Sasha why she believed this, she said things like, 'I just got that impression' and, 'It's because they are better communicators than me, more interesting'. Sasha's evidence supporting her insecurity was all coming from her own interpretation of the world. In turn, her interpretation of the world was driven by her beliefs. Rob telling her that he wasn't attracted to women for this reason did not change the fact that she believed it. Sasha's reticular activating system (the system within all of us which filters our attention, so we focus on the things that reinforce our beliefs) was working in overdrive. To help Sasha, we had to find ways to make her pay attention to evidence that contradicted her beliefs and show her that her thinking was too black and white.

The first step was to instil some new beliefs in Sasha. As Sasha felt like a failure because of her lack of education, we asked her to write down all of her successes and failures. Then we helped her look at her life so that she could see that it was full of learning experiences; none of it had been a waste. We showed her that she had done some things very well, and others not so well, and made sure that she understood that all failure is feedback. Now that Sasha has this wealth of experience, she can make the second part of her life more fulfilling.

Second, we had to alter some of her old beliefs to help Sasha understand fully that if Rob wanted to marry someone with a different background to her, he wouldn't have proposed to her. This was much easier with her new beliefs in place. We asked her to actively involve herself in conversations at dinner parties, with the same people she felt insecure about. Her challenge was to come up with an interesting point of conversation (ideally, one she knew Rob would also be interested in) and record the events in a diary.

Sasha's confidence increased and she was no longer torturing herself and Rob because of her insecurities. She took up some educational courses, in areas that she was interested in. Most importantly, she accepted who she is and accepted that Rob loves her for who she is. We knew we had been successful in bringing this couple back onto the marriage path.

Andy and Liana have been happily married for more than ten years. Now in their late thirties, they look like a couple who are still dating: joyfully chatting, laughing and holding hands. Their personalities and backgrounds couldn't be more different.

Andy is an introvert who is interested in science and football, and Liana is a total extrovert who is interested in sociology and the theatre. Andy comes from a large, loving family and, as the only son, he had lots of privileges. His parents worked hard and sent Andy to good schools. Liana comes from a troubled family and she grew up on her own. She chose to continue studying, without any encouragement from her family, and built a good life for herself.

When they met, Andy was a wealthy man and Liana had a steady job but not much money in her account. They were introduced at a friend's house and Liana talked about people and the world all evening. Andy was impressed by her knowledge, her energy and her interest in the world and in life. Andy lacked that same energy and was rather shy. On the other hand, Liana liked his modesty and shyness; she was always meeting men who were 'show-offs, loud and uninterested in the world around them'. Liana also felt safe with him, as she had been let down by her alcoholic father.

Andy and Liana were married six months later and now, ten years into their marriage, they are still extremely happy together. They are both aware of, and accepting of, each other's differences and they have never tried to change each other. Instead, they fill each other's gaps and shortcomings;

as a team, they excel at what they are best at. Andy is still an introvert, but with Liana he goes to parties and events; she is his 'extroverted self'. And Liana has found her soul mate, a devoted man who is there to support her and who encourages her to develop.

Unlike some of the couples we see for help, Liana and Andy have retained their own interests and individuality: the things they loved about each other at the beginning of their relationship. However, they also know when, and how, to compromise and they are fully supportive of each other, helping each other to be 'the best they can be'.

They are two very different but flexible people who learned, very early on, that love and commitment are the most important things in a successful relationship. Andy and Liana are both very willing, and very well equipped, to put constant work into their relationship and ensure it stays strong.

PART NINE: Expert opinion – case studies and answers to relationship questions

This part of the book contains letters and enquiries that we at Seventy Thirty have received over the years, and how we have resolved them.

75. My partner's insecurity over my success is spoiling our relationship

'I earn more than my partner, as I run my own beauty salon, and he often makes comments about women overtaking men career-wise and how house husbands are "copping out". I wonder if he's jealous of me or feels insecure, but I don't know how to change things.' – Julianne

Men are wired in such a way that it feels natural for them to be the breadwinner. However, modern life has changed the balance of relationships and women are becoming increasingly independent and successful at holding down a good career and still looking after the kids and the home.

Your partner may see how wonderful you are at managing your life and not know what his own role is, or should be. Think about why you need and want to be with him;

emotional support, sex, fun and someone to make you feel soft and feminine every now and then?

Men need reassurance that they are needed. The next time you have a bad day, talk to your partner, ask for his advice and make him feel valued.

Focus on the sexual side of your relationship. Make sure that you have fun together and that your mind is as much on him as on spending time with your daughter or running your salon. Involve him with day-to-day decisions about your daughter, so he feels that he plays a role in her life too.

Let him pay his way. Don't put up barriers by trying to be independent. You are right to think about your daughter's needs as well as his, but how about taking some steps to make your home feel more shared – you could redecorate together, or buy some new furniture together.

76. My boyfriend finds it hard to deal with his emotions

'I am worried about my boyfriend as he finds it hard to deal with his emotions and I think that he might be depressed. He has seen a counsellor once but does not want to go back. I feel so helpless; do you have any idea how I can help him?' – Lucinda

There is no easy solution or quick fix to issues like this. It is important to be a supportive partner, especially if you suspect your boyfriend may be suffering from depression, but it is also important that you take care of yourself. In this situation, it is important that you and your boyfriend surround yourself with loving and supportive family and friends. Many people will only access the professional help they need when they are at a point where they feel ready to talk about it. Sometimes the best you can do is show them that they are loved and you will be there for them when they are ready to talk. Try to spend quality time with him; encouraging him to speak about his emotions and hearing his fears can be very powerful sources of support, even though this may leave you feeling frustrated at times. In order to help him to take some responsibility for his emotions, ask him what support he needs from you at this point in time.

Supporting a loved one can be emotionally draining, and it is important to remember your own needs as these are also of great importance, especially if you feel that you are one of the main sources of support for your boyfriend. You may want to think about accessing support for yourself, as this will help you to process your own feelings and to stay strong. As you become more empowered to make the decisions that feel right for you, your boyfriend may be inspired to make the changes that are right for him.

77. Finding love again

'I am so fed up with facing everything on my own, but do not know how to change things. My selfish husband left me after 17 years of marriage. We had three beautiful children who helped me a lot in coping with life on my own. They gave me that extra bit of energy and motivation. The problem is that now my children have grown and gone away. I am 59 and I feel that I am on my own. All my friends are married and very much settled. I have no single girlfriends, so my social life is non-existent. Do you think it would be worth trying to find love again at my age or should I just accept and learn to cope with my singlehood?' – Melinda

For Melinda and the many other women and men who find themselves in this kind of situation, the overwhelming feeling is of being alone and worried about the future.

Will I ever find anybody? The good news is that it's never too late and, yes, you will.

Now start making the changes you need to achieve this. Start by listing everything you are grateful for. A good way to visualise this is to get a piece of paper, write 'Thank you' at the top and list the things that have made your life better. Start as small as you like – your breakfast cup of tea will do. The next thing is to forgive. This is not for anyone else's benefit but your own – forgiving your husband will allow you to have closure and to move on. Take the focus off what you *lack* and start asking what you really *want*.

It is time, in short, to become more 'selfish' yourself. Tell your children and your friends that you want to make some changes. Ask them to help you come up with ideas for areas in your life they think you should change. Ask them if they know anyone they could introduce to you. There many ways to meet suitable partners; you might meet someone in the supermarket, out on a walk, at your local church, on your street, in the DIY store, in the local café, or by taking up a new hobby. You can also try joining a matchmaking agency, which is a much safer and more effective way of meeting people than dating websites.

Dress up. Put on make-up. Brush your hair. Make yourself walk out of your front door. Put on some lipstick, hold your head high and give yourself a goal of smiling at least one new person a day.

78. Why am I nervous about dating?

*'I am very nervous! I was married for 34 years, from the age of 20, and I am not yet confident enough to tackle dating. In fact, it terrifies me! How will I be able to enjoy life again?' –
Bella*

Finding yourself single again after a long-term relationship ends is naturally going to be a little scary. However, the important thing is not to let your concerns and fears prevent you from moving on and enjoying another healthy, successful relationship.

First, it is important to allow yourself adequate time to fully get over your previous relationship. A key factor is being able to think about your ex-partner in a neutral way. Of course, you will have some very strong feelings initially, but it is important to acknowledge these feelings and accept them before eventually letting them go. If you still find yourself feeling bitter, resentful or sad, then it's clear that you have not yet fully let go of your emotions for your ex-partner and you are not yet ready to fully commit to someone new.

By being able to accept what has happened, and not blame each other, you will be one step closer to achieving closure. It can be difficult not to think, 'If only I had...' or, 'It all started when...' but such thoughts are destructive: you can't turn back time, and the important thing is to move on in a positive way.

79. How to avoid arguments

'My boyfriend is very rich and successful, and we have been together for two years. I love him deeply, but we often fight and I am worried he will split up with me. Please help me to control the arguments.' – Stephanie

Why do you argue with your partner? Once you understand why certain things bother you, you will be able to manage your temper. At Seventy Thirty, we will show you how to be diplomatic, how to avoid rows, and how to control your anger.

Two of the people we have helped are Elle and Alex. Elle is 27 and beautiful; she is dating a 35-year-old millionaire named Alex. Yet while Elle is an extrovert who likes to party and have a good time, she is very insecure. If Alex doesn't call when he says he will, she becomes very upset and thinks that he must be more interested in his work than he is in her. If Alex forgets to say 'I love you' when he leaves for work, Elle thinks he doesn't love her as much as she loves him.

After spending some time with Elle, and doing a 'stock check' of her life, it became clear that her relationship was not the only area of her life in which insecurities existed. Elle had stopped focusing on her career when she met Alex and had instead diverted her attention to making him happy. Now she relies on him financially, and also only works when he asks for her help with a project. Elle thought that this was what she wanted, but she is very unhappy and refers to feeling as though she has 'all her eggs in one basket'.

The real cause of Elle's insecurity in the relationship related to her own lack of direction in life. Alex had previously dated women with careers, and Elle knew that her successful career in dancing, alongside her confidence, was one of the reasons that Alex was attracted to her in the first instance. Now, Elle doesn't have those things, and she believes that Alex wants someone who does. Surprisingly, it transpired, after questioning, that Elle also believes that she has sacrificed these aspects of her life for Alex in order to make the relationship work. Elle was confused ('fuzzy') and increasingly argumentative towards Alex ('I can't help it, I seem to just have a bad thought in my head and it starts from there. I know it's not fair on Alex and I can sense that he is becoming fed up with it, but that just makes it worse').

To ensure that Elle could visualise her problem, we asked her to draw it. Elle drew a person with two paths in front of them. Both paths led to a picture (which, she said, symbolised 'things not working out' between herself and Alex). We asked her to draw a picture on the same page that represented the two of them being very happy together (she drew a brighter picture of the two of them and, interestingly, they were working on something together). Elle was then asked to draw another path in front of her, one which would lead to a positive picture, and to place flags on the path showing us where obstacles would be.

This work helped Elle to see her problems more creatively and to be open to successful outcomes, all the while knowing that there will be obstacles on the path.

Elle worked with us on examining her beliefs around choice versus sacrifice and also to examine some of her thought patterns, differentiating between false insecurities and reality. We then worked on helping Elle build her own goals, congruent with both what she wanted for herself, and what she wanted for her relationship. Finally, we gave Elle some tools to take away with her, so she could perceive situations more objectively.

Women such as Elle would benefit from a few neuro-linguistic programming (NLP) tools and some advice on cognitive behaviour patterns. For example, remember, he is not late because he doesn't love you. He is simply late because he is busy; otherwise he wouldn't be a millionaire, would he?

80. Why doesn't he want to get back together?

'I hooked up with this guy while on holiday over ten years ago. Crazy good time … amazing chemistry. But since we lived in different cities, we both went back to our "normal" lives. We ended up hooking up again about four months later … great times! We really enjoyed each other's company, both in and out of the bedroom, and ended up dating steadily for almost a year, but the distance became very hard for us to manage. We broke up, mostly because I wanted more of a commitment from him in terms of our "future" (damn biological clock!). So, my big question is: why doesn't he want to get back together?' – Rosanna

It sounds as though Rosanna and this gentleman had a lot of chemistry.

Chemistry is an amazing thing: it is totally unpredictable and outside our control. It is usually chemistry that gets a relationship off the ground. To say chemistry is powerful stuff is an understatement. It can alter our perception and make us try and fit with people who may not otherwise be compatible.

The fact that your relationship didn't move forward as you had hoped the first time might indicate that, while the chemistry between you was very powerful, there wasn't the right fit between the two of you beyond that. It also seems that, as he is still unwilling to commit himself in any real way to you, this is a warning sign that he is not willing to invest in the relationship any more than superficially. The blunt truth is this: if he genuinely was interested in a relationship, he would prioritise seeing you rather avoiding you.

If you really want to know where you stand with him, ASK him! He is the only one who has the answers. Don't fret about asking him for some clarity. You deserve to know where you stand.

81. Should I stay or go?

'I was with a guy for a year. He wanted us to get married but my father refused, because my boyfriend didn't go to university and my father thought he wasn't educated enough for me. but we decided to end it because we had several fights in the last four months of our relationship. However, we haven't managed to stay away from each other. We have been trying to get back together now for almost nine months but it's no use; we can't let go but we can't stay. He said the problem is that he is emotionally

drained; he loves me very much and wants to stay with me, but he doesn't know how to deal with me any more. I blame myself every day because I treated him very badly while he gave me the world, and now I am trying to fix things but I feel helpless. We tried taking a break, but it didn't change how he feels.' – Arianna

You say you want to make this relationship to work but you point out some obstacles that you see as immovable. It's confusing when our head and our heart disagree. It sounds like you have two things to do. The first is to make your decision. The second is to *stick to it*.

I was struck by two things in your letter. Not once do you say you love him. You say 'he loves me very much and wants to stay with me, but he doesn't know how to deal with me any more.' You also said: 'He wanted us to get married but my father refused because of his lack of education. I can't move in with him because my family will never approve.'

It seems that his lack of education is a major obstacle for you, as well as your father, since you don't seem to want to challenge your father's decision. You also say, 'I blame myself every day because I treated him very badly while he gave me the world and now I am trying to fix things but I feel helpless.'

We don't treat the people we love 'very badly'. It seems your motivation in staying in the relationship is to please him and because you feel guilty. Unless you truly love your boyfriend it is better if you both move on. You have both tried to walk away so it's clearly something that is on both your minds.

However, if you do love your boyfriend and you feel you could be together in a way that is positive and hopeful, try taking a step back and looking at it in another way. Instead of asking, 'How can we fix this?', imagine the relationship is successful and loving and visualise this in as much detail as you can. What has changed? How have you changed? How has he changed? How has your time together changed? How do you treat each other? How has your relationship with others changed, including your families? Ask your partner the same questions.

Having visualised your ideal future together:

- Discuss this with your partner and see if you share the same vision of a perfect relationship or if you want different things from each other.
- Discuss whether you both agree with the changes that need to take place to make this a reality.
- Assess whether your future vision is realistic and achievable by taking into consideration your values, goals and social/family group.

Remember, the outcome is not inevitable. You and your boyfriend have a *choice* about whether the relationship works. However difficult a choice is, it is still a choice.

If you choose to make the relationship work, you may have to address some things within yourself and with your family, which may be very tricky. However, remember that no matter how difficult it can be to make and then stick to a decision, it is always better to make a choice and move forward in a positive way than to stay stuck in a self-destructive rut where you repeat the same mistakes over and over again.

Making and sticking to a decision frees you to find the things in life that you need. So when the decision starts to feel tough, remember there is light at the end of the tunnel, and it will lead you to a future that is right for you.

82. Are we just friends?

'I like this guy. We have been close friends for some time and we flirt a lot. I told him indirectly that I liked him, but he just laughed it off without acknowledging my feelings for him, and I am not sure if he pretended not to understand or just did not understand. He says he doesn't want a relationship and I am not sure if that is for my benefit. He told me that he has a crush on another girl and I encouraged him to ask her out. I feel hurt and very bad. I do like him a lot and we talk daily but I don't know if I should wait around to see if we ever get together. Help! What should I do?' – Suzanne

A recurring theme that arises when Seventy Thirty is approached for advice is 'communication'. We know that it is hard dealing with powerful feelings of attraction when there is no clear reciprocal signal from the other person. You have tried to express how you feel and to seek confirmation of your feelings. However, apart from not being clear or direct enough to get a straight answer, it seems you have not fully prepared yourself for the scenario in which your feelings are not reciprocated.

Take a moment to think about why you were so indirect in expressing yourself. Did you fear rejection? Were you worried about losing your friendship? Do you lack self-confidence?

There is no easy answer, other than asking him again in a forthright manner. Ask for a clear answer. Men are not mind readers. Try not to send mixed messages; you do not want to confuse the situation further, especially as you have feelings towards him and you want him to understand them. For example, encouraging him to ask out another girl after a very weak attempt at explaining how you feel sends conflicting signals. It is possible he might have thought that you were not seriously interested in him or that you were only flirting. It is possible he did pick up your signals and is not interested. It's possible that he mentioned the other girl because he was trying to gauge your reaction to indicate whether you will reject him.

Do you want a relationship, or something more relaxed that may or may not evolve into a relationship? It's important that you know what you are hoping to achieve. If he is not interested in you romantically, you should think in advance about what this means for you and how you will handle it.

Whatever the outcome, at least you will know where you stand and you can move on. It will also give you the confidence and the tools to be more direct in the future.

83. Making the same mistakes again and again

'I seem to keep making the same mistakes again and again when it comes to the men I date. While I see my friends in loving relationships with men who look after and support them, I can never seem to find this for myself. My first love was scarred from his childhood and always seemed down; I gave him my all to support him, even though my own childhood was not that much better. I did so for five years but eventually became so drained that I had to leave. I resolved then to find a partner who could support me too, rather than it always being the other way around. I promised myself that I would not try to fix another person from within a relationship, but then I found myself dating an artist with no income and trying to coach him to better his prospects! My most recent relationship ended after 18 months because my partner drank too much, and despite all my efforts I was unable to help him come out the other side, so I left. I am nearly 40 and want children. I really don't want to waste time any more or keep finding myself in the same situations like my life is Groundhog Day. *Please help.'* – Tamara

It's clear how hard you have tried to do the right thing in each relationship, and also to leave when it became untenable. This shows strength of character and you should be proud of yourself. However, you also say 'my own childhood was not that much better' in relation to your ex, who you say was 'scarred' by his childhood. It sounds as though it was very difficult. It seems that you need someone to support you and to help you unlearn unconscious patterns that are directing you towards certain partners. Although you try to be strong, it sounds that you may have learned that you are not 'worth' anyone more stable and loving to date.

This is not uncommon. Many adults will repeat the same negative relationship patterns over and over again. However, these choices are not inevitable; patterns can be consciously broken. For example, take mothering or trying to 'save' partners. Many people in your position have had a difficult childhood relationship with at least one parent. Typically, as a child, they would have felt threatened by at least one significant figure who was a strong and dominant character. For example, a child with an aggressive father may go to great pains as an adult to avoid a relationship with a man where they could be put in the same position. Therefore, they will be drawn to relationships where they feel needed, even if this is in the context of a partner's self-destructive behaviour, such as drug or alcohol abuse.

Given the difficult time you experienced as a child, it may be worth getting in touch with a professional therapist who can help you work through your childhood and give you the tools to go forward in a positive way for future dating.

84. How best to suggest a pre-nuptial agreement to a partner?

'I am getting married soon, and as I am wealthy (inherited wealth, but I also run my own businesses) I am seeking advice on how I should best suggest a pre-nup to my future wife, without her getting upset. What do you suggest?' – William

When suggesting a pre-nuptial agreement to a partner it is always best to be absolutely honest. For instance, don't skirt around the issue by talking generally about people you know who have used them, as this may make your partner think that you are trying to manipulate the conversation. It is probably best to introduce the idea openly and honestly by explaining that you are thinking about a pre-nuptial agreement and why you find it important.

Tell your partner your reasons for proposing this. It is important to emphasise that you are not suggesting you do not trust your partner, but rather that you are seeking security and reassurance for yourself that your assets/wealth are not the reason your partner is with you. Make it clear that pre-nuptial agreements are not about whether you can trust the other person; it is so that both partners know exactly where they stand, so that money concerns will not become a factor later in the relationship.

It may also be a good idea to compare a pre-nup to a marriage contract. When two people promise to love and respect each other in a wedding ceremony they are entering into a binding agreement; the only difference is that the pre-nuptial agreement is legally binding and refers to finances rather than love, emotion or fidelity.

Only by being absolutely honest with your partner and discussing this issue in a frank and open manner will the two of you feel able to absolutely trust each other. A well-defined pre-nuptial agreement should help both partners to feel secure and validated within the relationship and ensure each can move forward, confident in the knowledge that they have a relationship built upon genuine love and companionship rather than wealth or entitlement.

PART TEN: Lesbian dating and relationships

85. A guide to lesbian dating

With homosexual relationships often seen as more 'disposable' and shorter-lasting than their heterosexual counterparts, it is no surprise that lesbian women face challenges in their quest to find quality connections. When looking for a new partner, it is prudent to think about what is attractive about you, as well as what attracts you – remember, potential partners are on the same path as you are!

Attractiveness

To lesbians, what makes a woman attractive is simply being who she really is. No smoke or mirrors. No games or riddles. This may mean having a true understanding of her own identity and her emotional and physical needs, or having a clear idea of her life ambitions, her career plan, being financially stable and feeling independent and settled. It is at this point that she can consider who would be a good long-term match for her. When thinking about attractiveness in a partner, it is vital that she acknowledges and recognises her own good points. These can then be linked with good potential matches to ensure an element of compatibility.

Sexual attractiveness

Lesbians are often attracted to a partner in whom they can see aspects of themselves, both in and out of the bedroom. It is no secret that men place great importance on a potential partner's physical attractiveness, whereas women, and especially lesbian women, do not hold these same values.

For some lesbian women, sexual attractiveness is often about 'mind over body'; it is about trusting each other, confidence and affection. Communication is key with sexual attractiveness – do not be afraid to talk, discuss, explore and enjoy.

Finding similar values

Quality connections are formed based on openness and honesty, which are two of the most sought-after virtues when searching for romantic connections. Lesbian women place great emphasis on the parallels between their own life values and their partner's virtues, understanding how these links can create successful, long-standing relationships.

Having an understanding of her own values is therefore attractive to potential partners, who will also be able to draw these comparisons while dating and looking for love.

Growing together

Women are deeply focused on creating life partnerships, meaningful connections and, subsequently, growing within their relationships. They are adept at recognising their own flaws and can use their partner's positive characteristics to help themselves grow and develop. It is important to be passionate about building your relationship together, allowing it to change over time – no relationship just slots together like a jigsaw; instead, it is about enjoying the challenges along the way.

The balance of power

As relationships continually develop, so the balance of power changes. Although most lesbian relationships would like to claim an element of egalitarianism, power – and the subsequent division of roles – is unequal in nearly half of all lesbian relationships.[14] Women who are in an unequal relationship report feeling less satisfied and unsettled in it, with a higher chance of anticipating relationship problems in the future than their equally balanced counterparts.

To achieve an ideal relationship, there should be a healthy balance between dependence, relationship involvement, role-sharing, financial contributions and even 'equal interest' in each other. However, conflict in relationships has been highlighted as merely 'growth trying to happen', as the power shifts from one partner to the other. Lesbians in particular feel the need for an equal relationship, with the added pressure of balance to eliminate aspects of the butch–femme stereotype.

---

[14] Cladwell, M.A. & Peplau, L.A. (1984) The balance of power in lesbian relationships. *Sex Roles, 10*, 587–99.

86. Dating etiquette

When it comes to dating, we all think of the traditional scenario; the gentleman picks the lady up, arranges where to go for a romantic evening and picks up the bill, before dropping her off with a goodnight kiss – sounds like most chick flicks, right? However, in modern-day dating, especially lesbian dating, those traditional norms disappear.

With lesbians, the modern dating etiquette that we discussed earlier applies: stay off your phone, remember your manners, be polite, treat her as you would like to be treated… but some lesbians may have some additional worries when dating, and we discuss these below.

Who arranges the date?

The stereotypical assumption is that one lesbian will take the 'butch' (male) role, and one will be more 'femme', assuming the female role in the budding relationship, but modern-day dating isn't as black and white. It is perfectly acceptable for either of you to arrange a date, no matter if you identify as butch, femme or somewhere in between.

Remember, *confidence* is an attractive attribute in a partner and is placed higher than physical attractiveness in recent psychological studies. With this in mind, making the first move to arrange a date is never a bad move, and is actually a positive indicator of successful relationships. Although by asking a woman out you are possibly opening yourself up for rejection, you are also opening yourself up to the opportunity for success and getting to know someone better.

Taking it in turns to arrange dates is a nice way for both parties to feel appreciated and attractive. If you arranged the last date, do not automatically assume she will arrange the next one, however. Sometimes she might need a confidence boost herself or a nudge in the right direction. Asking her if she would like to see you again opens up communication about dating so you can casually ask, 'Would you like to arrange where we go, or shall I?'

Top tip: If you are asking her out on a first date, it is polite to call instead of text or message. This shows you are serious, outgoing and confident. It also prevents a long delay between asking and her answering, which can be misconstrued.

'Who's the man?'

The eternal question of *who is the man?* has an element of truth. For some lesbians, particularly femme–femme couples, there may be some initial concern about the male–female roles usually played out. Who opens the door for who? Who walks who home? Who initiates the first kiss? These are unwritten rules in heterosexual dating, with the man usually assuming responsibility, but who takes responsibility for these during lesbian dating?

A woman is very good at reading and responding to situations – if you feel that your date might not be as comfortable taking on some of these roles, and you are, then show her. Remembering our first point that confidence is attractive, assuming these responsibilities does not mean that this will always be the case. There are always options for role reversal within lesbian relationships – roles are fluid and ever-changing. So, just because you assume responsibility on this date doesn't mean she will not take the initiative and assume these responsibilities next time you meet.

Who picks up the bill?

A fair way of deciding who pays the bill would be to assume whoever initiated and arranged the date would pay. This means that, when deciding where to go, you can tailor your choice to your budget, whether this is a five-course meal in a fine restaurant followed by a top-end theatre production, or a romantic homemade picnic in the park.

Can I take you out on a date?

Don't suggest that you expect her to pay or pay half. If your date insists on paying, which is courteous of her, say she can get it next time – giving her the signal that you would like to meet again, as well as the opportunity to spoil you later on.

If you move on after dinner to a bar for more drinks and your date paid for dinner, offer to pay. It is only fair to take it in turns.

Etiquette about the ex

Leave your baggage at home. Some women have a bad habit of bringing up past relationships in new relationships, but a good rule is not to discuss ex-partners. Constantly referring to your ex can suggest that you are still hung up on her and create an element of hostility.

Neuropsychological studies have found that thoughts and associations with ex-partners cause the body to feel actual pain. When starting fresh with someone new, it is therefore important to refrain from dating in the same places you visited with ex-partners, and not to identify similarities between ex-partners and current partners. By doing so, you can unintentionally create associations between past and present partners. If you find this happening, good dating etiquette means you should take time out. Allow time for healing before continuing to date.

The follow-up

Following a date, it is courteous to contact her and thank her for the evening out – even if you arranged it and paid for it, or didn't enjoy it that much.

It is often hard to continue texting or messaging after a date – who makes the first move? By making reference to something that happened during the date, you are showing you are interested in her and the time spent with her, allowing for conversation to start and develop towards when next to meet.

If you enjoyed the date but you don't want to take the relationship any further, be honest. Someone who has manners and is thoughtful automatically has date etiquette, and it allows you to nip any unwanted relationship in the bud.

87. Dating rules

Dating can be a minefield at the best of times. Acknowledging a few rules throughout the dating process can help you find your right match, who might just be your Ms Right!

1. Dating outside your contacts list … and your friends' contacts lists.

It is a hazard for a lesbian to date within her friendship circle, as one gay woman admitted:

'This is usually because it is harder to meet new lesbians, so naturally females are drawn to their groups of gay friends or friends of friends. Often these circles are very incestuous, which can cause animosity and jealousy.'

Try and meet women externally to widen your dating circles. Sports groups are a fantastic way to meet like-minded people and to keep you healthy and active – exercise also helps your psychological wellbeing, allowing you to keep your body and mind healthy.

Another way to meet local lesbians is to visit lesbian bars or lesbian nights on the gay scene, where you can enjoy the freedom of knowing you are in a social setting surrounded by females of the same sexuality. This is one hurdle your female heterosexual counterparts may not have considered – when in a bar, how do lesbians know who is gay? By being in a specific social setting you are opening yourself up to the chance of meeting new people – potential friends *and* potential partners.

You can also look for social groups (such as theatre and arts groups, musical groups, or hobbies such as beer-making or cookery classes) specifically targeting lesbians. These are often area-specific, which means you will be able to meet someone local to you.

As the lesbian community is quite small, however you meet your date, try not to date someone you know, or who has dated one of your friends in the past.

2.   Don't rush: keep your options open

When choosing who you'd like to date, think carefully. What characteristics do you admire or require in a partner? What do you find attractive? What do you dislike? Do you have certain time restraints with home or work life that wouldn't match someone who also has the same commitments?

It is easy, as a lesbian, to think you haven't much choice when choosing a partner, therefore settling for someone who might not fit the bill to avoid being alone. One of the biggest mistakes is rushing into a relationship with the wrong person, inevitably ending in heartache and a messy break-up. By being realistic about who you are looking for and being true to yourself, you will have more chance of long-term relationship success – after all, you cannot commit to travelling 300 miles to see a partner if you work 12-hour days or have commitments at home.

Although it may sound unfair to go on numerous dates, by doing so you are keeping a healthy mental state. Lesbians are known to suffer from 'U-Haul syndrome': becoming too attached to partners and moving too fast in relationships that are often not right for them. This isn't healthy for your psychological wellbeing, and dating numerous people means you don't get to know any of them too quickly, allowing you to maintain neutrality and independence.

If your feelings grow for each other past the initial dating stage, never date more than one person at once. Always be upfront and honest if you do not feel the same.

3.   Be transparent, upfront and honest

Pretending to be something you are not, or forging interests to build a connection with your date, will never work in the long term. Be honest to yourself and to her during dating. This will allow you to build stronger connections and foundations for your relationship to grow. If you do not match, then recognise and acknowledge your differences to see if they will hinder a possible relationship.

Transparency in relationship goals is also vital when looking at relationship success. Psychologists found that incompatibility is a significant predictor of an unsuccessful relationship and, as lesbian relationships often move more quickly than heterosexual ones, *honesty* and *transparency* are vital from the beginning to ensure you are each aware of how the other person feels.

4. Do not play emotional games

Women are complex creatures. No matter how old you are or what stage of dating or a relationship you are at, you will consider unintentional game playing. This may take the form of not rushing to text her back because she takes a while to reply, refraining for asking her on a second date because you arranged the first one, or not saying 'I love you' first because you want to know she feels the same before showing you are emotionally attached.

Playing games is hurtful and pointless. For instance, if you are annoyed she doesn't contact you regularly, not contacting her in response will not allow her to recognise this pattern of behaviour. Speak about your feelings – communication and honesty are the only way for a relationship to grow successfully. So, if you are in love with her, tell her how you feel. If you are annoyed, be honest and tell her why.

An increasing proportion of the lesbian population are using specific services to meet potential partners, such as singles nights, online dating and matchmaking. Singles nights, which allow you to mix with groups of women you know are available, may seem like a good option if you are confident. As online dating grows more popular, it has become more attractive to many people: it allows you to search and speak with women who may match your physical preferences, educational requirements, background, and so on. Although online dating has been criticised for being impersonal, it does allows you to build a rapport by communicating online before you decide if you would like to meet in person. Remember that communicating too much prior to meeting creates a sense of overkill – the build-up, discussing your lives and interests in too much detail, can leave the date unsatisfying.

Matchmaking provides an alternative option and is available to individuals who don't have time to waste scrolling through hundreds of profiles. It is tailored to those who would like more of a personal introduction to a fewer number of exceptional matches, with a better rate of success. A professional matchmaker will understand your goals, values, interests and lifestyle, matching you with someone perfectly suited to *you*. You will then have the freedom to speak and meet up to explore where the date may lead you.

88. Body language

A recent study found that only 18% of women could detect when someone is flirting with them, in comparison with 36% of men being able to recognise flirtatious behaviour.[15] That is just one out of every five women... As women are notoriously hard to read anyway, when we then think about single lesbians, we wonder if this statistic could be even lower.

So, if you want to know if she is flirting, let's look at body language. Body language signals differ from person to person – a woman who identifies as butch may not display the exact same body language as a woman who identifies as femme, so when trying to read her signs, think about where on the spectrum she might identify.

Her body and movements

Body direction: When she is speaking to you, does her torso face towards you or away? If she is interested in you, she will face you, subconsciously displaying the way you would view her if you were intimately involved.

Look at her feet: are they pointed towards you or away? If standing, are her legs slightly parted, showing she is strong and powerful? She may show more masculine body language traits; she may make her body look bigger, which is

---

[15] Hall, J.A., Zing, C. & Brooks, S. (2014) Accurately detecting flirting: error management theory. The traditional sexual script, and flirting base rate. *Communication Research*. At: https://news.ku.edu/2014/06/03/flirting-hard-detect-study-finds.

understood to be attractive, giving you a sense of feeling protected. Now look at her feet. If they are pointing directly towards you, it signals attraction and flirtation – that her interest is in you, rather than anyone else.

Her position: If sitting, crossed legs – one knee over the other for a more feminine match, usually left leg over the right – might be seen as closed body language if coupled with retraction of the torso (sitting or leaning away from you), with crossed arms showing an element of emotional withdrawal. However, crossed legs with knees/top leg facing you is a positive indicator of attraction. It shows she is engaged and interested in you. If she touches her thigh, smoothing her trousers or skirt, this is also a flirtatious movement, signalling she wants to draw your attention to that area.

Look at where she is in comparison to you. Is she standing or sitting just on the boundaries of your personal space, or closer? This can indicate she wants more physical contact with you. If she leans in when she speaks to you, this shows she is attracted to you and she wants all your attention solely on her. At this point, notice if she lowers herself when she speaks, does she bend over to rest an elbow on the bar or table? This shows that she is letting you take control, submitting herself to you and allowing herself to be more emotionally available.

Movements: a woman will generally gently touch her erogenous zones when romantically interested, such as her lips and neck. These areas become more sensitive when attracted or aroused.

She may expose her wrists towards you, and she may play with her hair or touch her face. This is both a masculine and feminine response; running her fingers through her hair or allowing her hair to be displayed over her shoulders.

You will also notice those flirtatious little touches differ from woman to woman – a feminine aspect would be to gently touch you. If she withdraws her hand and brings it to her chest or face, it shows additional attraction. A masculine approach might be to touch your wrists with her thumb and forefinger, showing dominance, protection and power.

Take a moment to think about your own body language when you meet someone you like. Often lesbians will mirror each other's body language subconsciously to show compatibility.

Facial language

If a woman is romantically interested, when listening to you she will subconsciously (and unintentionally) flare her nostrils and sit with her mouth slightly parted. She may possibly gently bite or lick the inside of her lips, which is to not only draw her match's attention to her mouth as a sexual entity, but also because when aroused a female's mouth becomes dryer.

When speaking, her facial movements will become more active and animated. Raising her eyebrows, widening her eyes, fluttering her eyelids (a feminine trait) and smiling while speaking show her enthusiasm and interest. It is also a subconscious technique to keep you interested and focused just on her, not other people in the room.

Eye contact

Eye contact is key in knowing if someone is interested. If you have met a potential match in a bar or social group, you will notice her making eye contact with you at a distance. If a woman holds your gaze for more than three seconds and returns it within a few seconds, you know she is interested.

When speaking face to face, notice if she takes a feminine approach by looking into your eyes, glancing away and returning her gaze immediately after; she will probably also touch her face or hair during the second gaze. A masculine approach may be keeping eye contact firmly, not looking away from you, showing confidence and dominance.

89. Why do lesbian relationships move so fast? The truth behind U-Haul syndrome

Within the lesbian community, relationships have a tendency to move quickly. From the first date, to saying 'I love you', to moving in together, then buying a house and saying 'I do' – the time span can range from just a year onwards. This has become known as *U-Haul syndrome*, a term originally used in lesbian culture in North America.

The psychology behind U-Haul syndrome

Females are biologically designed to create deeper connections to ensure they will love and look after their young. This connection also applies to their romantic attachments, with the help of the hormone oxytocin. Oxytocin is released when falling in love, during orgasm, touching, childbirth and breastfeeding. Oxytocin is released in both men and women, but it has been found to affect the sexes differently. Of course, oxytocin is important in bonding and attachments, but a study found that in men it has also been found to improve the ability to identify competitive relationships, and in women it has improved the ability to identify kinship. Generally speaking, women are genetically predisposed to create attachments. In female–female relationships, we are looking at two beings whose hormones are solely charged for kinship. Oxytocin, inducing the feeling of love, can become addictive, meaning the relationship itself can become an addiction.[16]

Social psychology also plays a part in U-Hauling. As children, girls imitate weddings, using tea towels or net curtains for veils, we carry babies in our jumpers, we push prams with our pretend bundle of joy sitting proudly under the blankets. Society teaches us that our goal in life is to achieve a successful relationship and then have children. It also suggests that this should be through a traditional male–

[16] Fischer-Shofty, M., Levkovitz, Y. & Shamay-Tsoory, S.G. (2012) Oxytocin facilitates accurate perception of competition in men and kinship in women. *Social Cognitive and Affective Neuroscience, 8*(3), 313. DOI: 10.1093/scan/nsr100.

female relationship. In lesbian relationships, we may therefore expect to feel an element of inequality and lower self-confidence.

With biology creating an addiction to your partner, coupled with societal norms and the element of lowered self-confidence, U-Hauling suddenly becomes less a theory and more a reality.

Spending too much time together?

You may think, 'That's rubbish, I'm not addicted to my partner!', but take a step back and look at your past relationships. Do you notice a pattern in seeing each other very frequently, particularly at the beginning of each relationship? Did you make excuses not to see your friends so you could see your girlfriend? Did you get to the stage where you did not have anything to talk about? Did you find yourselves having less in common as time went on?

Lesbians move so fast because they spend a lot of time together. Being inseparable means you do all the things a heterosexual couple usually does in a year or so, in only a few months. Consider also that being inseparable means you have no time to have new, individual, experiences. Without these experiences to discuss, your flow of conversation can dry up as you have no new facts or stories to hear about one another. Without a night or two apart a week, you are creating a world which is solely inhabited by you both; this puts an extortionate amount of pressure on your relationship and your partner.

Are you currently in a relationship? Take a step back and ask yourself if you have had time apart recently. Is your relationship consuming your individual identity? Have you become a 'we' and 'us' rather than an 'I' and 'me'? Spend some time apart; you'll notice self-growth and romantic growth. After all, absence makes the heart grow fonder.

90. How to make your relationship last

You have found that seemingly perfect person, but you worry about ensuring your relationship's longevity. Or maybe you feel you *had* the perfect person and you're left pondering over 'the one who got away'.

First, remember that there is no magical cure for romance problems. Although there are many common themes, relationship success is unique to each couple. However, it is evident that it takes time and commitment for a successful relationship: you have to work at it.

The long-standing joke about lesbians loving cats will probably be familiar to you, so when thinking about your relationship, think about 'CATS' – just not the kind that wake you up at 3am meowing.

C – Communication

'My girlfriend and I lie in bed on a Saturday morning, after one of us has pulled the short straw, got up and made a bacon sandwich – one of us inevitably drops a dollop of

ketchup – not brown sauce – on the white bed sheets or spit outs tea while giggling … and we just chat … we discuss everything.'

Communication is key to relationship success. Talk about your concerns and worries. Talk about your memories, your life stories and your future goals. Without communication, you lose your connection.

Make time to communicate – this could be while cooking dinner together, out on a walk or having a lie-in at a weekend. Wherever it is, talk, discuss, share, chat, dream and plan. This allows you to create inside jokes, nicknames and little 'us' things that only you and your partner understand. You can think about your future together and get excited about things you want to do, both together and individually.

Laugh – having a sense of humour, laughing at yourself or laughing together is important. This does not mean letting your partner be the brunt of the jokes, but knowing when to use humour to keep your connection alive.

Apologise – if you've done something wrong, apologise. Recognise your faults and embrace them. If you deny responsibility, you run the risk of creating cracks in your relationship that can become larger problems.

Acknowledge – if you notice that it's always your partner who's doing the washing-up, taking the bins out, making the bed … acknowledge her. Thank her for doing things that make life nicer. Small gestures of romance help her to feel acknowledged: little notes under her pillow, Saturday morning breakfast in bed, or sending flowers to her at work. Also, remember to ask your partner if she is happy doing these things: discussing shared duties and opening communication is key here.

A – Alone time

Remember you are an individual and, as such, you need time alone. Continue your individual hobbies, see friends, spend time with your family. It is normal in a new relationship to throw yourself into it and spend a lot of time together. However, as the relationship develops, remember that time apart allows you room to breathe. As lesbian relationships have two female parties, it is hard not to include your partner in your group of female friends – after all, she is your friend too. If you met your partner through friends, you may find that your circle of friends is her circle of friends, creating a larger issue when trying to socialise independently and triggering jealousy or resentment if you arrange to see your mutual friends alone. Try to encourage her to see her own friends and continue her sports or hobbies. Time apart creates a foundation for more discussions, and absence makes the heart grow fonder.

T – Time together

Although time apart is important, time together is vital. This doesn't mean doing everyday things; it refers to making a special arrangement where you ditch the iPad, leave the iPhone in your pocket and go on a date night. Once a month, take it in turns to plan an evening out – meet at the venue and always make sure you're visiting somewhere new, which will allow you to create memories. If you are worried about conversation, see a comedy show or watch a live gig – go somewhere with atmosphere. If you want intimacy, go to a cocktail bar, or lounge at a spa.

S – Sexual Interaction and compatibility

For relationship success, it is essential to make sure you are sexually compatible. If one of you is less sexually active, problems will loom. She may feel like she is a 'sex pest' by coming on to you, feeling rejected, left feeling unsatisfied and wanting your sexual attention, or she may feel unattractive – even if she feels otherwise loved. Take notice of your partner's sexual needs and talk about them openly. If you do not feel like having sex, tell her why.

Keep your sex life alight by being willing to engage in new experiences. So-called 'lesbian bed death' (a term coined by US sociologist Pepper Schwartz) can be avoided by introducing new ideas in the bedroom: new positions, watching pornography, choosing, buying and using new sex toys, having sex in different venues or rooms of the house. If you are having problems in the bedroom, agree not to engage in any sexual act for three weeks. In this time, do not get naked in front of each other. Make a date in the diary for a dinner at home three weeks later; give yourselves enough time to relax in the bedroom afterwards, and re-explore each other's bodies. Making a sex date will help you to regain the initial physical excitement and help you to re-engage in spontaneous sex later on.

91. My partner is distant from me

'I am a 46-year-old woman who has been with my partner for 20 years. We own a lovely home and both have successful careers. Recently she has been distant from me, lying about where she is and staying out late. She seems to be spending more time with our friends alone, when we would usually always see them together. When I confront her she tells me it's nothing, but I feel like she is not telling me the truth. I have asked her what the matter is, but it seems to be pushing her further away. I've told her that I am beginning to feel crazy and that I feel like she is not interested in me, or us, any more. How do I get us back on track and get the spark in our relationship back? I can't bear the idea of losing her and starting again.' – Miranda

After being in a relationship for so long, it is understandable that you are feeling confused and lonely – after all, your partner is probably your best friend too, someone who you would usually turn to for advice and support, and suddenly she isn't there to help you.

Upon reflection, notice you said, 'How do I get us back on track?' A relationship is a two-way street with both of you needing input, commitment and love to keep it going. It sounds as if your partner is not making the same amount of effort that you are to keep your relationship strong. She is excluding you and at the same time spending time with others when you feel threatened and need her support. On top of this, it appears she is avoiding discussing your concerns and worries. By being dismissive, she leaves you feeling as if your worries are trivial and you're being unreasonable for needing to discuss them. This leaves her open to continue behaving in a way that is hurtful and inconsiderate of her long-standing partner – you. Is this acceptable, or what you want from a long-term relationship?

Remember that communication is key. I understand that, by speaking to her, you feel that you may be pushing your partner away, but remember that by not voicing your worries, *you* are being pushed away. Open the lines of communication; ask her to sit down and talk to you. A good tip is to write all your worries down beforehand and go through them methodically with a clear mind. Feelings aren't usually methodical, so this technique can help you structure your conversation and identify what is upsetting you. This allows you to address your concerns more logically and will help you to feel more in control, giving you the confidence to realise that you deserve more.

From here, you have a few options. First, stay in your current relationship and continue on the current path, which is leaving you feeling isolated. Although I am no mind reader, I presume this would not be the option you would pick, as you are already unhappy.

Second, you could stay in your current relationship and seriously discuss the option of *change*. Discuss her feelings, as well as your own, and get a good understanding of how you are both feeling. Make a positive plan to move forward; arrange a date night every week where you take it in turns to arrange a special evening for the other person, and spend quality time together, but also arrange a night where you are free to regain your independence and see separate friends or engage in activities or hobbies. By having this time apart, you will have new stories to tell each other. If you can both make the effort, your relationship may reignite its spark, giving you a greater sense of balance and allowing you to be happier.

Lastly, you could go your separate ways. I wonder if you fear being alone, or perhaps fear meeting someone new after putting many years of love and effort into your current relationship. When love isn't working out, it is always painful and emotional, especially when you feel that you're the only one who has been making any effort. Remember that sometimes the pain you feel initially when realising a relationship isn't right will be outweighed when you find a partner who is right for you and will treat you in the way you deserve – or even when you find your gorgeous, confident self again.

Lesbian relationships, by definition, are more intense for biological and environmental reasons. As lesbians are more likely to engage in deep relationships that are isolating and all-consuming, finding your independence is essential for your own happiness. It might even help you rebuild bridges, whether with your current partner or with old past friendships who can help you rebuild your social connections, allowing you to find 'you' again.

Maybe you could sit down and answer your own letter. If a friend had come to you with the same worry, what would your advice be?

Whichever path you choose, make sure you talk to your partner with confidence and assertiveness. This will help her realise that you mean business and you are not willing to be treated this way, or feel this way any longer.

92. My family doesn't approve of my relationship

'I am from a very close Christian family who do not believe in homosexuality. I am a lesbian, and this is a huge issue for them. I came out to them a year ago but I have been with my girlfriend for four years. We are in the last stages of buying a house together, but my family just do not approve of us both being women and it's making me doubt my relationship.' – Rebecca

I wonder if you doubt your relationship because the relationship is wrong for you, rather than due to your family's feelings towards it – after all, you did not say you doubted your *sexuality*. Ask yourself, would you date other women if you and your partner were to break up?

The next step is to sit down alone and separate your feelings for your girlfriend from your feelings for your family. One good technique therapists use is to ask you to imagine you have lost your girlfriend; imagine you have split up. Imagine the break-up and play out the story in your mind like a film – write down the emotions you feel. After this, do you feel a greater sense of appreciation when you see her next? This might be a clue to how you are subconsciously feeling.

However, it is important for you to understand if your family's feelings are what is creating a sense of doubt. Have you considered that there are two factors here that could underlie how your family views your relationship?

As you highlighted the possibility of homophobia or not understanding your relationship with your girlfriend, I wonder if you have seen the 'I'm Sorry' campaign run at Chicago Pride 2014, where Christians apologised to the lesbian, gay, bisexual and transgender (LGBT) population for how the church has treated them? It is inspirational, and shows us that religion can be accepting of all. I am making the assumption that you were also brought up in the Christian faith and known within the church? If so, could you seek advice from your church, which may be able to mediate between you and your family? If not, would your family see a support mentor with you?

You have been in a serious, committed relationship for three years and failed to tell them. It is hard for any family to find out their daughter is gay, but not telling them might have caused them to have feelings of distrust and rejection. It is possible that your family feel you excluded them from a big event in your life and now they find that difficult to discuss or rectify. It would be good for you to verbally acknowledge this and discuss it with your family – ask if they do feel this way, and if they would feel the same if you were dating a man? I think you need to remember that your confidence will breed confidence.

As you doubt your relationship, I think the first thing you need to do is work out how you feel. *Be honest with yourself*. The stress of buying your first property might be weighing on you a little at the moment so bear that in mind and try to detach yourself from the worries of the house and your family while you think about your relationship and if it is right for you.

PART ELEVEN: Gay dating and relationships

93. Internalised homophobia and relationships

In a relatively small period of time, much has changed for the gay community. It was only in the 1970s that 'being gay' was removed from the Diagnostic and Statistical Manual for mental health problems. In the UK, it is now legal for gay people to marry.

In order to promote such change, first we have to create awareness and exposure, which helps to change attitudes and beliefs, which drives (and therefore changes) thoughts and behaviour.

'If my father had seen me holding a guy's hand ten years ago, he would have probably thrown the nearest object at us to break us apart. Before he could see us, I would probably have dropped the guy's hand like a hot potato, in shame. However, when my father saw me holding a certain gentleman's hand recently, he gave us a weird approving look and said, "You're both my sons"... at which I dropped my partner's hand, embarrassed by my father.'

Change is certainly evident; the father's homophobic attitude has changed and the son is comfortable being gay around him. However, the son's internalised homophobia has also changed and he is more comfortable being himself, with his partner.

The external changes (in society, in government policies, in the workplace, etc.) are bringing gays closer to their quest for equality; they are creating an environment where they are free to be themselves. However, the internal changes, accepting themselves as gay, lesbian or bisexual, are equally, if not more important. Is there still a residue of internalised homophobia? How does that affect gay relationships or the ability to find one?

Many people brush off the idea of internalised homophobia as ridiculous. However, do you feel comfortable being with a very effeminate man in public? Are you 'out' at work? Are you 'out' to your family? Do you take your partner to work events? Do you take your partner to see your family? On a scale of 1 to 10, how anxious are you when you think of these things?

Overcoming internalised homophobia has been seen as part of a gay person's self-development along the path to *self-acceptance*. As young people growing up in a society where heterosexual lifestyles are the norm, young gay people often experience a disconnect between what they desire and what they have learned to be correct/right/normal. Coming out is usually seen as the first milestone towards a healthy self-image. However, feelings of internalised homophobia can persist long after coming out, even if one is integrated into the gay community and is having gay relationships.

Internalised homophobia can have a negative impact on one's relationships and ability to find one. Frost and Meyer

2009,[17] when looking at internalised homophobia and relationship quality, found that internalised homophobia:

- has a negative effect on one's self-concept or self-esteem, which can lead to problems with general wellbeing and even mental health;
- has been found to lead to problems with 'ambivalence, relational conflict, misunderstandings, and discrepant goals' in relationships;
- has been found to affect gay men's sexual intimacy;
- has been linked to loneliness – one may have less social support, particularly from other gay people.

Internalised homophobia is present at several different levels on a psychological scale. On one side there can be a reluctance to hold hands in front of colleagues and, on the other, greater side there is depression and self-loathing. For the latter, it is advisable to consult a therapist who can help you develop positive self-regard, combat depressive symptoms and help develop healthy social support systems (Frost and Meyer 2009). However, on the less extreme side, we may have what is perhaps better referred to as *stress about being gay*. The term 'homophobia' is currently unpopular because it is not a phobia, but perhaps it also sounds extreme; when we think about stressors about being gay it easier to see that we may all have a few of them.

---

[17] Frost, D.M. & Meyer, I.H. (2009) Internalized homophobia and relationship quality among lesbians, gay men, and bisexuals. *Journal of Counseling Psychology*, 56(1), 97–109. doi: 10.1037/a0012844.

Effeminate gay men often feel that they are unattractive because most gay men want to meet someone who is 'straight-acting'. Does this in itself suggest stress about being gay, for both the effeminate man and those seeking someone who acts straight? Putting this pressure on potential partners to be straight-acting means that they feel they have to act straight in order to be attractive.

The level of *outness* is associated with how comfortable one is with their sexuality and therefore correlates with internalised homophobia – being out at work, out to one's parents, out to friends and family. In a relationship, if one partner is out to all of the above and wants to include their partner in their extended social network it might be important that this is reciprocated. If not, one's partner can feel insecure about the relationship – 'I am a secret, I am not good enough, you should be proud to be with me.'

Self-assuredness is something that is very attractive to most gay men. If one is stressed about their sexuality or about being gay, this can be a turn-off. Being comfortable with yourself is a sign of security and wellbeing, which is appealing.

In London today, as in many major cities around the world, being gay is no big deal. However, many people have grown up in environments where being gay was not the norm, so it is not unreasonable that, at the core, gay men may still have some unhelpful residual stress about their sexuality. We don't have to label it, but we can recognise it and confront it, which will hopefully lead to healthier relationships and healthier individuals.

94. Why is it hard for gay men to find love?

Some single gay men feel that a well-angled selfie of a fit torso is given greater weighting by other gay men than their values, goals and personality (not to mention their face). Single gay men often come to me feeling that online dating is far too sexualised and focused on hooking up, so they doubt that any like-minded compatible men are out there who want a long-term relationship.

This sexualisation has been aided by sites such as Grindr, which, after exploding on to the online dating scene in 2009, quickly established itself at the forefront of the gay online dating sphere as an all-male, location-based social network. With more than six million men now using Grindr in 192 countries and growing, its popularity can't be ignored.

Apps like Grindr have allowed a convenient, fast and inexpensive way of connecting with other gay folk in close proximity. They also allow anonymity, exploration of sexuality and a way to browse our neighbours from the comfort of our own sofa. However, such apps are also criticised for being just about sex, and being too focused on the 'visual' (one photo and a very brief description), giving rise to body image problems.

The majority of gay men who come to Seventy Thirty are looking to settle down into a long-term relationship, with the potential of marriage, children, homes, pets and growing old with their love.

Connecting with people via social media certainly has its benefits and can even reduce depression and loneliness, in the same way as socialising in the flesh. However, having apps on our phones is changing social patterns of communication and courtship and having a negative effect on our social skills. So maybe it's time to lift our heads from our phones, breathe in the air and view the real world for a change.

Why is it difficult for gay men to find love?

Growing up in a heterosexual society with a lack of gay role models can lead to difficulties in modelling a healthy relationship. Having a troubled past linked to being gay can give rise to mental health problems. There is also literature on internalised homophobia and how it affects partner selection. On a practical level, there are fewer gay people out there; one might only feel safe approaching another guy if they are in a gay environment to avoid the awkward situation of approaching a straight guy.

We still have a long way to go, but in London attitudes have changed rapidly. We can all find a partner if we want to, but often we make excuses to protect our egos and the self-fulfilling prophecy keeps us single. If you really want a partner and you can't find one, try harder!

What do gay men want?

The same thing everyone else wants.

Confidence: gay men are more attracted to other gay men who they find confident, can feel comfortable with and able to communicate with in a strong and purposeful manner that mirrors their own level of confidence. Self-confidence can be elevated and projected in many ways on a physical level, through paying particular attention to grooming, clothing and maintaining a healthy lifestyle.

Power of proximity: gay men who are comfortable in their own skin and with their own sexuality are attractive. Focusing on your positive features, making eye contact, speaking clearly and listening attentively projects confidence and demonstrates a desire to understand and get to know another individual.

Sense of adventure and freedom: gay men are attracted to people who demonstrate a desire to fulfil their sense of adventure and also have the ability to be courageous when exploring their sexuality.

Attraction: gay men tend to be attracted by people who find them – or seem likely to find them – attractive: 'The faces we like best are the faces that are looking our way. The eyes that we are mesmerised by are the eyes that are looking into ours.' Gay men do not desire those who seek instant gratification or whose sexual urges are rebellious or unrealistic, but rather those who are able to demonstrate emotional intimacy, stability and a mutual attraction.

Openness and honesty: gay men tend to place intense emphasis on these traits, as well as a strong sense of pride and self-worth when it comes to their own life perspective and expression of this. The ability to open up to another gay man and create the ideal environment for him to express himself defines integrity of character and is highly valued, respected and appreciated by gay men who are searching for a life partner.

So what should gay men do to find love?

Spending too much time checking phones and apps inhibits social interaction. Anxious people are more likely to have their heads down, looking at their phones, when on their own in a bar; confident people are more comfortable standing on their own. Keep your head up, notice your surroundings and acknowledge the people around you.

Fear of rejection is always the major inhibiting factor in finding love. Many people spot potential suitors, hoping that they will be the one to initiate contact. Approaching someone and showing interest in them is often flattering to the other person, and it's unlikely that they will be cruel to you if they are not interested. Stop letting opportunities pass you by. When you go out, make sure that you strike up a conversation with at least one person; start with someone who you are not that attracted to, and work your way up to the guy who currently causes your IQ to drop by its square root.

Get out there – take some time to focus on yourself. Think of the things you want to do, such as learn a new language, take up a new sport, etc. Focusing on your interests means you'll end up socialising with like-minded people who could potentially be a love interest or could introduce you to a love interest. Taking up a hobby, such as joining a gay sports club, is a great way of meeting other gay people.

Be appealing – if you don't think you are attractive, you're probably not. Think about what you need to do to feel more attractive. When you *feel* more attractive, you will *be* more attractive.

Don't spend too much time online. The more profiles you flick through, the less likely you are to find a date. Flicking through lots and lots of profiles that don't match will make you feel despondent about your chances of finding love, plus if you are always seen online, you will get a bad reputation (if you log on to a dating application or an online dating site and see the same profile online all the time, you would view that person negatively. You might assume that they are promiscuous, desperate, do not have a social life or no one wants to date them).

I could list a hundred pieces of self-help advice that you already know about how to find love, but instead I recommend that you stop creating obstacles to finding love, and become proactive. It's empowering to take your life into your own hands. Who cares if you are rejected once or twice along the way to success?

95. Fear of rejection

One of the biggest things that prevents us from finding love is that niggling fear of being rejected. 'What if they say no? What will that mean? I'm ugly. I'm not good enough.' For some of us, being rejected confirms those negative beliefs we have about ourselves. 'If it happens once, maybe that's OK, but if it happens again then I *must* be ugly.'

Fear of rejection may have an evolutionary purpose, as the need for approval keeps us in the protection of the group, and we are stronger in a larger group than we are alone. A certain level of fear can be helpful in some situations and, in survival terms, keeps us alert and ready. However, when this is not needed for survival or when we feel a disproportionate amount of fear for the situation we are facing, it can be limiting. In an anxiety-provoking situation, we go into fight or flight mode. If we are more prone to flight, we may avoid situations that cause anxiety, which then exacerbates our anxiety.

The good news is, if you are not putting yourself out there for fear of being rejected, you can easily overcome this. In heterosexual relationships, traditionally, the gentleman is expected to approach the lady (of course, some women will happily approach a man). However, in gay dating situations, there are no rules, so who is going to approach whom? In the ideal world, you would spot each other from opposite ends of the bar and gravitate towards each other before engaging in an intimate discussion about life until the conversation leads to an eagerly anticipated kiss. Well, that does not happen very often; sometimes you may notice each other but neither of you makes a move, or he might not notice you at all, in which case, either you make a move or he won't know that you exist.

Challenging negative beliefs

We have already noted that fear of rejection protects our ego from harm. Recognise the negative thoughts in your head – 'He's going to laugh at me', 'I'm going to embarrass myself', 'I'm not good enough for him' – and replace them with more positive thoughts: 'I'm just saying hello', or 'Even if he is not interested, I hope he feels flattered'. We have a habit of thinking the worst and talking ourselves out of situations, or even behaving in a way that reinforces that negative belief.

Feeling more self-assured

Gay men are attracted to other men who are self-assured and quietly confident. Therefore having the confidence to approach someone is attractive in itself. We don't want rejection to confirm the negative beliefs we hold about ourselves. But, actually, we shouldn't give a random person in a bar, who doesn't know anything about us, any power over our self-image. Learning to be more self-assured will mean that you feel confident in yourself and rejection from a stranger will not have as much impact on your ego.

How to handle rejection

If a guy rejects you, the best thing to do is be polite and gracious. That way he will feel flattered by you and appreciate your attitude. If he does act in a nasty way, then he's a fool, and you have had a lucky escape!

Facing rejection

Feeling anxious about a situation can lead to *avoidant* behaviour; however, avoidance simply reinforces the fear. The best way to handle anxiety is to face it head on. When dealing with anxious clients, one method that has proven very useful is a gradual exposure to the feared situation, while learning techniques to deal with it. The same thing can be applied here.

Considering the advice above, think about situations where you could meet potential partners and write them down, from the most anxiety-provoking to the least. Start by practising meeting people, exposing yourself to situations where you meet people that cause you the least anxiety, and then work your way up. Use business networking events to help you meet people, where everyone is a stranger and there to meet new people. Get used to meeting new people for business and then transfer these skills to meeting new people for a relationship.

Exposure is the best way to build confidence. The more you practise approaching people, the easier it becomes. You may experience setbacks, but don't give up. Fake it till you make it! Soon you will be conducting yourself with such social grace that everyone will want to talk to you.

96. Gay men are bitches!

Bitchiness, usually seen as a female trait, can be adopted as part of one's personality and played where appropriate.

'Mean girl' behaviour is prevalent among gay people, and it seems to fall into two categories: the street-smart, feisty, fireball attitude and the rather posh 'I'm above it all' attitude. Interestingly, as the struggles in the gay world lessen and therefore the internal conflict in identity development lessens, this attitude is becoming less prevalent.

With many gay men having to go through life challenges to gain self-acceptance and social acceptance, self-worth can be low. They may therefore put up a wall and develop defence mechanisms. The harder the struggle, the stronger the defence. Bitchy behaviours are often reinforced because the social group rewards the behaviour with laughter or respect. Through social comparison, gay men can also elevate themselves within their group by putting others down. It is sometimes considered light-hearted fun, rather than being malicious, but we cannot deny it exists.

Is the bitch attractive?

Being bitchy is not attractive. No one comes to Seventy Thirty looking for a partner saying, 'I want someone who's bitchy.' In fact, most people who come to me say that they find it unattractive and they are ashamed when they adopt this attitude themselves. Most people, heterosexual and homosexual, view this attitude with distaste.

Both masculine and effeminate gay men often seek masculine characteristics in a partner. No one likes a mean girl. There is growing homophobia in the gay community towards effeminate men. Their gay peers feel that they are feeding the stereotype of gay men, and therefore camp is not cool. However, this attitude towards effeminate gay men is feeding the 'bitchy' defence mechanism.

Carrying bitchy attitudes into a relationship can also be very problematic. There is often some conflict when you start seeing someone, which helps the relationship develop; bitchy, sarcastic attitudes or behaviours are maladaptive and can lead to relationship breakdown.

Overcoming the bitch

Bitchy behaviours can be very difficult to break, particularly if you identify as being bitchy and have created a role within your social group as 'the bitch'. Even more difficult, the act of being a bitch can be a defence mechanism for internal insecurities. 'Let's divert attention from me; let's make others scared of saying anything about me and let them know that I am in control.' On the other hand, some people just enjoy going out and making 'innocent' comments about others for the sake of a giggle.

First, you will have to want to change and recognise that your behaviour is not helpful. This has probably become habitual, an automatic response, so you will need to think about social situations where you are being a bitch and practise substituting your bitchy behaviour for something more helpful. You will slip up; someone will come along and give your inner bitch an opportunity you can't miss. But keep at it. If you have to say something, say something nice – try to compliment people instead of being bitchy. Don't say everything that comes to your mind; use a filter.

Also, think about your social identity. Other than being a bitch, what positive things are you known for? Perhaps you're the funny one; if so, make jokes at your own expense rather than others. Think of other ways in which you can make people laugh.

Learn to control your emotions; do not suppress them. Sometimes bitchy behaviours are the easy response when you feel challenged, and suppressing your emotions is likely to result in an explosive reaction disproportionate to the situation. Think rationally and logically; learn to be assertive rather than bitchy.

In the long term, perhaps it's time to focus on the insecurities that 'the bitch' protects you from. Perhaps when you start showing the real you, you will receive confirmation that you are a great person and that people love you, and not the comments you make about others.

97. Moving in with your boyfriend

It is important not to get carried away with the romantic idea of moving in together, and to maintain a realistic perspective of the changes that you are about to embark upon. It can be fun, exciting, romantic, but may also be stressful and challenging. Your relationship dynamic will change and your day-to-day life will change. It is important to consider if you are both ready for this change and explore the practicalities involved.

Think about your motives for moving in together and what it means to you. Many couples move in together because it is convenient or cheaper, but this is no reason to shack up; you have to ensure that your relationship is ready for this commitment.

You should explore with each other your ideas and expectations of living together: are they shared and realistic? Remember that the little things always cause arguments, so be clear on how you intend to divide up the chores, paying bills, dealing with DIY, and so on.

Moving in together also means pooling all your belongings and furniture. How do you plan to do this? Are you prepared to get rid of your favourite chair because it does not go with the décor? Do you have similar styles and tastes and how will you combine them?

Finance is one of the major issues facing cohabiting couples. Before moving in together you should have a clear idea of how you will divide financial responsibilities and resources. In addition, you should be aware of each other's financial priorities – is it more important to spend your money on a glamorous holiday, or invest in a property?

Couples should always consider each other's long-term goals, which include relationship and individual life goals. Are you travelling on the same path and are you willing to compromise?

Do you really know what is important to your partner? Is their behaviour driven by their political beliefs, or their family's values? Do they have strong views on health or career progression, or are they more motivated by having fun? At Seventy Thirty, we matchmake through exploring values, because a relationship is more likely to survive time and conflict when the partners share similar values.

How long should you wait before you take the plunge? Why?

It is very important that the timing is right before moving in; however, this is different for every relationship. Generally relationships go through a number of stages, starting with the honeymoon period, before each person starts to show their commitment to each other. Relationships may then go through a power struggle or crisis period(s) before the next phase of the relationship, which is one of growth and rebirth.

The honeymoon period can last between a few weeks to a year; it is important that you don't take the plunge while you are still wearing rose-tinted glasses.

Often people move in together because it's more convenient to do so; it usually works out cheaper, as you can pool your resources. You might be able to share a wardrobe (providing he has good taste), you get to spend more time together and increase the intimacy of the relationship. However, this is no reason to move in. Be sure that if you do move in together, it is because you are in a secure and committed relationship, where you are comfortable and feel strongly compatible with your partner. You must both be ready and willing to take the next step in your relationship.

Make sure that you know your partner well enough. When living together, there will be plenty of opportunities for conflict. You should have reached a stage in your relationship where you have been through challenges together and you know how your partner handles conflict so you can find the best way of working through problems.

Don't move in just because it is more convenient or practical to do so, or because you feel your relationship is in trouble and this will fix it. It won't. The problems in the relationship will only be magnified under the same roof.

How do you know when the time is right?

If you are in a secure and committed relationship where you are comfortable and feel you have a future with your partner, it might be the right time to consider moving in. However, ensure that you are both ready and willing to commit to each other to be able to work through any issues that may arise within a changing relational dynamic.

What are the pitfalls of rushing into cohabiting?

Fools rush in! Most couples who move in together too soon and have trouble living together end their relationship.

While speaking to people about relationships, I often hear how chemistry and emotion can take over and drive the relationship forward without the couple taking time to think things through logically. Some couples want to move to the next level of intensity, when sometimes it better to take your time and enjoy each stage of the relationship – because there is no going back.

I hear of couples who move in together expecting the passion in the relationship to escalate. However, when two people live together the passion in the relationship may start to decrease over time. Therefore, moving in too soon can be at the detriment of your sexual relationship and you have to work to find ways to keep the spark alive.

People often take their co-habiting partners for granted, so moving in together before your relationship has had the chance to develop can result in a break-up, because it may not be strong enough yet to withstand the new challenges.

How can we make the transformation from dating to cohabiting a smooth one?

It is important that you have open communication and ensure that disagreements or discussions are solution-focused, rather than problem-focused. Take the time to really listen to each other.

Practice makes perfect. Try staying over at each other's homes first, or going on a long holiday together, as this might help you get a better idea of what is like to live together.

Don't rush into buying a property together; perhaps try renting first.

Put some time aside for date nights with each other so that you get to spend some quality time together.

Understand each other's boundaries and respect them.

Remember that your relationship will work well if the other person feels valued. Focus on your partner's positives – what is he good at?

Before you move in together, what ground rules should you set? Everyone will have different ground rules depending on their boundaries and values. It is therefore important to explore what is important to each of you so that you know what mutual boundaries to set. It is usually a good idea to have ground rules around finances, chores, social lives and independence.

Maintaining independence is key – ensure that you take time out for yourself; you should always have some alone time and you should try to maintain your other social relationships. After all, if this does not work out, you might need a shoulder to cry on.

98. To have children – or not?

Having children can be a contentious issue for many couples and can be one of the major sources of conflict in a relationship. This is because people have deep-rooted individual values associated with what makes an ideal relationship and what values they want to instil in their children. A relationship with conflicting value systems is unlikely to last.

A child is for life and not just for the good times, so having a baby should not be used as a crutch for a failing relationship. Having a child greatly impacts upon the dynamic of a relationship, and both partners need to work together when it comes to raising a child, so that they are able to cope with the challenges that lie ahead (and there will be many).

We worked with a couple, David and Patrick, who have a five-year-old boy, Shane. They adopted him even though their relationship was turbulent. Having Shane temporarily brought them closer together, but soon their conflicting values meant that their arguments escalated and their differences were amplified. David worried about the parents at school accepting him as a gay dad, while Patrick worried about his son being bullied for having two dads. They also worried about their child asking questions about their situation: 'Why do I have two dads?' If their relationship had been stable before they had a child, they would be able to cope much better. However, because their relationship was already in trouble, having a child had only exacerbated the situation.

There are many important issues to consider when a relationship breaks down, and having time out can provide a useful space for reflection and can help you to see your relationship in a different light; what was working and what wasn't? How did it make you feel? What would you do differently the second time around? A relationship should take into account each person's relationship goals and individual goals.

People often think about how their life will be when they have a child; however, they should also consider the child's needs. Both parents need to be committed to bringing up and providing a child with a secure and loving home. When you have a strong family support system, you can deal with almost anything.

Would you be truly happy if you never have children? Would your partner truly be happy if you did have a child? It is important to maintain a realistic view of your relationship and to iron out any issues with your partner before you have a child. When one partner gives up their dream this can lead to resentment, which greatly impacts upon intimacy and communication within the relationship.

99. Should I get back with my ex-boyfriend?

There is no easy answer to this question. Only you can decide if this relationship feels right for you at this point in time. Why did you break up?

'I wanted marriage; he didn't.' You may want to explore why you want to get married. Is it the idea of marriage that attracts you, or is it to cover up the cracks in your relationship? Marriage is not a quick fix for a relationship that's already on the rocks. You should only take that step when you are both ready and willing, and your relationship is healthy, with mutual commitment, intimacy and passion.

First, you should talk openly about your expectations of marriage – do you both want children? Are your longer-term goals compatible? If you are living together, do you share household chores or argue about whose turn it is to load the dishwasher? It is easy to make assumptions, but you will only find out what your partner is thinking if you talk to him.

You need to be realistic and listen to what he is telling you, rather than hear what you want to hear. If he is saying that he never wants to get married, you must be willing to accept that this might not change.

You should bear in mind that gay marriage is relatively new. There are many men who never thought they would marry, and they may have developed negative beliefs towards marriage as it was not legally accepted. If this is the case with your partner, it may take some time for his views to change – if they change at all.

When someone wants to marry you, they usually show you that this is their intention. They will make you feel secure in the relationship by giving you signs that they want to build their future with you, whether that is buying a property together, having a joint bank account, saving together for the future or exploring potential wedding venues.

You may want to think about why you broke up in the first place and why he doesn't want to get married – is the issue about commitment, is it about feeling secure in the relationship, or does he just not believe in marriage?

In order for a relationship to last, a couple should have similar life goals, and both may need to compromise on these. You need to consider if this is a compromise you are willing to make. Would you truly be happy if you never get married? What does getting married mean to you and your partner? Can you find a middle ground?

Was this the only major issue in your relationship, or were there other things happening beneath the surface? It may help to speak honestly and openly about your feelings to try and understand your partner's point of view. What are their fears? Can you do anything to reassure them? Many issues can be resolved by communicating openly, as this helps to build trust and intimacy with your partner. However, if marriage remains one of your long-term goals then you need to focus on finding a man who wants the same thing.

100. We have nothing in common

At Seventy Thirty we matchmake based on core values since, when a couple has compatible core values, the relationship has the best chance of long-term survival.

It is important that you and your partner both want the relationship to work and are willing to make the effort to do so. Couples can work together to find something they both enjoy doing (such as taking up a new sport or hobby, or going to an evening class) or may prefer to start arranging regular 'date nights' when they can go out for dinner, go to see a movie, or have a romantic night in.

Often, when a couple say they have nothing in common, it is an indication that there is a problem elsewhere within the relationship, and this may be linked to communication.

If you are worried about not having anything in common, it is important that you are able to communicate openly with each other. Couples often say that they have nothing in common because they have nothing to talk about. Maybe you are spending too much time together, but not enough quality time? Although it is great to share common interests, it is important to maintain a sense of independence within a relationship. Couples don't need to do everything together, and it can actually help the relationship when you have your own interests and maintain a strong identity.

Relationship counselling can help you to explore some of these issues and underlying value systems. At times it may be easier to work on emotional expression in a neutral environment, and you may want to see a couples therapist together if you are both willing to work on your relationship. Sometimes individual therapy is also beneficial, as it can provide the space to heal from emotional issues.

Testimonials

'The real genius of Seventy Thirty is that it is exclusively tailored to respond to the needs of affluent people. Seventy Thirty's vast network of contacts across the dating scene work to introduce you to that someone special, and then it is over to you. Seventy Thirty's service is one that wastes no time and offers you the crème de la crème of the dating scene.'
Quintessentially

'Years ago, psychoanalyst Susie Ambrose helped a rich and aristocratic man to find the woman of his dreams. Today, he and his wife are bringing up their children in a happy marriage, and Susie is the CEO of a matchmaking business with a growing list of millionaire clients.'
Mayfair Times

'A growing number of deep-pocketed continent-hoppers are choosing to "outsource" the soul-sapping searching and sifting elements to relationship "headhunters" – dating agencies that only the affluent can afford, such as Seventy Thirty, whose offices are in Knightsbridge, in the shadow of Harrods. Seventy Thirty has seen a jump in membership numbers in recent years, something its staff attribute to customers "reflecting on what is important to them" during the economic turmoil – and relationships come high on that list.'
London *Evening Standard*

'Wealth is an indicator of success, but women at Seventy Thirty place more emphasis on finding a partner who is academically brilliant or creative.'
The Times Magazine

'Typically, successful people have ambitions and dreams, with the drive to realise them. They seek potential partners who can appreciate this dedication, are intellectually stimulating, sophisticated yet fun, and with whom they can enjoy their lives. But Seventy Thirty does more than just set professionals up on a date. Susie Ambrose finds that many clients benefit from services such as life coaching, image consultancy and date coaching.'
Director Magazine

'In the past, matchmaking was an informal means to connect potential mates based on factors such as cultural or social standing. In the present, the advent of technology has forever changed the landscape and effectiveness of this means of meeting a significant other. These digital dating systems have given rise to the professional matchmaker, and represent a major advance in the profession. Enter the world of luxury matchmaking with Seventy Thirty. Seventy Thirty is the first and most exclusive luxury matchmaking agency, offering a discreet and entirely exclusive service to affluent clients.'
Eat Love Savor

*'When one loves somebody everything is clear –
where to go, what to do – it all takes care of itself
and one doesn't have to ask anybody about
anything.'*

Maxim Gorky

**I hope you enjoyed reading this book, and I wish
you every success in finding a very special life
partner.**

Susie Ambrose

Printed in Great Britain
by Amazon

35914907R00153